The Grace of It All

~

Reflections on the Art of Ministry

The Grace of It All

~

Reflections on the Art of Ministry

F. Dean Lueking

THE
ALBAN
INSTITUTE
Herndon, Virginia
www.alban.org

The Alban Institute
2121 Cooperative Way, Suite 100
Herndon, VA 20171-5370

Unless otherwise noted, all Scripture quotations are from the New Revised Standard Version of the Bible, copyright ©1989, Division of Christian Education of the National Council of the Churches of Christ in the United States of America, and are used by permission.

Scripture quotations marked KJV are from the King James Version of the Bible.

Cover design by Signal Hill.

Library of Congress Cataloging-in-Publication Data

Lueking, F. Dean (Frederick Dean), 1928-
  The grace of it all : reflections on the art of ministry / F. Dean Lueking ; foreword by Jill Pelaez Baumgaertner.
    p. cm.
  ISBN-13: 978-1-56699-332-6
  ISBN-10: 1-56699-332-6
  1. Pastoral theology. 2. Church work. I. Title.

BV4011.3.L85 2006
253--dc22
                                    2006031638

        10 09 08 07 06   UG   1 2 3 4 5

*With gratitude to my pastoral
associates at Grace through the years.*

~

Contents

Foreword, *Jill Peláez Baumgaertner*   ix

Preface   xiii

1   Ministry as Art and Vocation   1

2   The Virtues of Ministry   13

3   Pastor and People   43

4   Turning Conflict into Ministry   71

5   Pastoral Rhythms   95

6   The Grace of It All   121

~

Foreword

George Herbert, the 17th-century Anglican priest
most well known for his collection of poetry *The Temple*,
had a very short pastorate. From a well situated family,
Herbert was educated at Cambridge, elected to Parliament, and
was well on his way to a brilliant political career when in 1630
he abruptly changed direction, taking holy orders and accepting the pastorate of the tiny country church at Bemerton. Four
years later he died at the age of 39, leaving behind a collection
of extraordinary poetry.

In contrast, F. Dean Lueking has been in the ministry for
more than 50 years, serving 44 years as senior pastor of Grace
Evangelical Lutheran Church in River Forest, Illinois. Like
Herbert, however, he received a stellar education, his many
talents leading him to occasional tangential considerations of
a career as a ballplayer or as a physician; but finally he chose to
heed God's call to the pastoral ministry. Despite opportunities
to serve as a seminary professor, Pastor Lueking remained faithful to his original call. Here in this volume of reminiscences and
insights gleaned over the course of his long career, he does what
George Herbert did in his collection of poems: reveals a deeply
committed servant of Christ, whose humility is intact even after
the most potentially head-turning of worldly successes.

In his poem "Aaron," Herbert takes as his model the first
priest, Aaron, the brother of Moses, dressed as God directed
in Exodus 28 with the signs of holiness, light, perfection, and
harmony. But Herbert feels unworthy, dressed as he is in the
old Adam's garb of profaneness, darkness, defects, and noise.
He remembers, however, that he puts on the garb of another
head, heart, and breast—that of Christ himself, who becomes

ix

his "only music," striking the old Adam dead, dressing him in brand-new clothes, and in such robes he calls the people to him, his "doctrine tun'd by Christ (who is not dead, but lives in me while I do rest)."

And thus the image of Lueking as I know him, having watched him for more than 25 years, learned from his careful and beautiful sermons, and in so many other ways benefited from his ministry to his parish. I see him in the regal vestments of the officiant at communion, at baptisms, at confirmations, at weddings, and at funerals. And I also remember his removing his priestly garb on Maundy Thursday to wash the feet of his parishioners. He is there, completely present, at times of critical need in the lives of his flock, and it is never Dean Lueking standing on his own authority, but Dean Lueking under the authority of Christ.

As a parish pastor Lueking writes this book for parish pastors, speaking frankly about his joys and his trials. He uses graphic illustrations from his daily life-describing, for example, the time he unhesitatingly tackled a burglar outside the church; or the sermon he had to give only once to make a point, beginning it with 90 seconds of uncomfortable silence. He speaks of the temptations of plagiarism or the lack of full honesty for the preacher. He describes the joys of sabbaticals and the challenges of retirement, which he has mastered by taking the advice of a friend and filling it with new opportunities for ministry to the global church.

When I think of Pastor Lueking, however, I see him where he seems to be most entirely himself: in the pulpit. "To be known as a preacher," he writes, "is in my experience to have no better identity." Lutherans do not believe that ordination is a sacrament, but we do believe that the preaching that follows ordination is, as Lueking puts it, "inseparable from Eucharist." As Herbert puts it, "in him I am well drest."

Aaron

Holinesse on the head,
Light and perfections on the breast,

Harmonious bells below, raising the dead
To leade them unto life and rest:

Thus are true Aarons drest.
Profanenesse in my head,
Defects and darknesse in my breast,
A noise of passions ringing me for dead
Unto a place where is no rest:
Poore priest thus am I drest.

Onely another head
I have, another heart and breast,
Another musick, making live not dead,
Without whom I could have no rest:
In him I am well drest.

Christ is my onely head,
My alone onely heart and breast,
My onely musick, striking me ev'n dead;
That to the old man I may rest,
And be in him new drest.

So holy in my head,
Perfect and light in my deare breast,
My doctrine tun'd by Christ (who is not dead,
But lives in me while I do rest)
Come people; Aaron's drest.

Jill Peláez Baumgaertner
Professor of English, Dean of Humanities and
Theological Studies, Wheaton College

Preface

TREASURE HAS BEEN GIVEN TO ME, ONE THAT I WANT to share. Having been a parish pastor for more than a half-century, I marvel at the sheer privilege of witnessing God's surpassing goodness, the grace of it all, at work in the lives of people. In these reflections on the art of pastoral ministry, I intend neither to romanticize nor to minimize the demands made on clergy today, but to encourage all who have a part in the pastoral calling.

We have much to share with each other from our daily experiences with the ups and downs of congregation-based ministry. In this format, the conversation might seem one-way. I write, you read. I talk, you listen. But I hope that doesn't make it a monologue. If my words on these pages can move your thoughts and imagination toward those you serve and the circumstances of your congregation, then a dialogue begins. It might affirm what you are already doing in some aspect of your ministry. Or you may argue with me about what I've suggested here or there. Or you might gain a new insight. Or, best of all, perhaps you will catch a glimpse of a larger vision of your ministry that comes not from me but from the Lord of the church. As such things happen, conversation is taking place, through me and those I serve to you and your people. I have long been the beneficiary of such lively conversations with authors I've never seen or met but whose writings have engaged me in spiritual and intellectual exchange that enriches me greatly. It's good to keep that sort of thing going.

I am a Lutheran. This is said not to build a wall but to offer a bridge to other members of the whole Body of Christ. I bring to this conversation the fruits and foibles of my 50 years of pastoral experience, 44 of them in one congregation, Grace Lutheran Church in River Forest, Illinois, a western suburb of Chicago. I believe I share with you an insight you also have learned along the way—that a congregation never stands still but in some sense is always both new and old, challenging and vexing, lively and dull, and, in ways both hidden and overt, amazingly heartening from year to year. In this regard I bring a huge indebtedness to other clergy and laity of other places and traditions, and acknowledge that indebtedness best by weaving into this conversation what I've learned from them. When I refer by name to this or that person to personify some aspect of ministry, the idea is to build crosswalks that fit the particulars of people and circumstances you know so well.

Talking shop with fellow clergy is and always has been important, informative, and enjoyable to me over the years. In some of the difficult patches of my ministry, those exchanges with colleagues have been much more than shoptalk. They have been life-giving to me in my need for a listening ear and an understanding heart. There is a beautiful phrase in the Lutheran confessions that speaks of "the mutual conversation and consolation of the faithful" as being of virtual sacramental status in experiencing what God the Holy Spirit accomplishes in such earnest give-and-take.

There is a shortage of this kind of parish-pastor-to-parish-pastor literary genre. I've puzzled over this lack through the years, regretting that such a wealth of hands-on experience and practiced theology doesn't reach print. True, all of us benefit greatly from those who write on pastoral ministry as seminary and university teachers. And many of us recall that among our best teachers were those who had congregational experience along the way or are still active in preaching and teaching in a congregation. Yet the dearth remains. The lack finally must be met by those who are in the thick of parish ministry—who believe, think, pray, and serve people of all sorts day in and year out, immersed in the wonder and befuddlement, the rigor and delight, the humdrum and astonishing surprises, the failures and achievements of the quotidian rounds of serving people in that assembly unlike any other, the congregation. It's made up of forgiven sinners who keep on coming together to worship God, to live Christ-given lives of witness in the world, and to build each other up for the high calling of mutual nurture and common witness by entrusting themselves to the mystery of the indwelling Holy Spirit.

The need is for pastoral writing that joins sound theology, biblically grounded in the mighty acts of God's judgment and mercy, with the realities of congregation and community in our world. Indeed, down through the ages God's people have always gathered in congregations, a fact easily unappreciated for its ongoing importance. Particularly in this day when a wispy, untethered spirituality tempts many to dismiss the church and any commitment to what is derisively called "organized religion" (a.k.a. a congregation of people composed of human beings unlike themselves), we are called to show and tell people what they are missing in that prosaic-looking gathering just around the corner. The need is for biblically sound and theologically informed reflection, offered without apology, that tells what happens among real people in real life when they keep on coming together for worship and mutual upbuilding in the congregation and then keep on going out as agents of God's mission in the worlds they occupy between Sundays.

Here, then, is an effort in that direction, a testimony from one pastor and congregation, in company with Christians nearby and around the world. This pastor and this congregation have lived through seismic changes in church and society during the past half-century, and I speak from that perspective.

A guiding biblical passage that has been paramount in my years of ministry is from Paul to the Ephesians, that "the gifts [God] gave were that some would be apostles, some prophets, some evangelists, some pastors and teachers, to equip the saints for the work of ministry" (4:11-13). That expansive phrase joins the ordained ministry inseparably with the daily ministry of God's people in the world. It has given me my identity and daily purpose as a pastor since it was opened up to me in my seminary days. The grace of its freshness and the power of its truth have not faded or faltered since that time. I'm still learning its depth and breadth in this time when I'm retired, an awkward term that never quite fits the continuing ministries that many of us keep on doing in some way or measure. It motivates me as I write this book, an offering that might help equip pastoral colleagues who in turn equip God's people for ministry in their daily worlds. The frequent references to pastor/laity connections here are proper to the subject of ministry in its fullest sense. Neither is complete without the other; both need each other.

When one steps back to think about it, it is astounding that God would put his power to save, gather, renew, and send out his people through something as vulnerable and risky as a word, the word of the cross no less, that Paul names as sheer foolishness to the unbeliever. Yet such a fragile vehicle as a word, with God speaking through it, becomes nothing less than his wisdom and power that save and renew all who believe. To fallible mortals like us he entrusts this treasure. He does so with grace abundant! The miracle, therefore, is that this ministry exists. We are partners in it. And we can now converse about it.

1

Ministry as Art and Vocation

THERE ARE VIOLINISTS. AND THEN THERE IS ITZAK PERLMAN. What is it that makes the difference? There's an art to making magnificent music à la Perlman, an art made up of genius, practice, sacrifice, endurance, discipline, enjoyment, and something indefinable that brings all these things together. When one listens to a genius violinist, it's hard to sum up the effect on mind and spirit of what is heard. It's something akin to what Augustine had to say about time—I know it when I see it but can't define it when asked.

And so with pastoral ministry. There's an art to being a pastor. It begins with the call of God. It deepens and expands as an art through motivation, experience, creative imagination, discipline, courage, striving for excellence, risk, setbacks, successes, knowledge, wisdom, imitation, prayer, growth—the list goes on. In short, it comes about through loving God with the whole heart and mind and soul and the neighbor as oneself in all the varied scenes and situations of the pastoral life.

One thing is certain. The art of ministry is not an end in itself. That's affectation, the stuff of outward piety and dress, airs of superiority, "chancel prancing," the "stained-glass voice," and insufferable stuffiness. The art of ministry is seen in those who are least conscious of practicing it. It's more caught than taught. Like the art of parenting, hitting a baseball, repairing an engine, or sewing a designer dress, the art lies in making it look easy. Or in the case of pastoral ministry, the art lies in showing it to be genuine as one goes about the calling of making goodness attractive, making faithfulness something much to be desired.

More than we tend to realize, pastors must do lots of things and do them well. We're generalists in the sense of needing skills for speaking, teaching, listening, thinking, guiding, leading, and the like. Interesting, isn't it, that such a general variety of required skills turns out to be a specialty—as general practitioners are specialists in medicine. There is no substitute for the discipline of hard work in developing the art of ministry. While divine grace motivates this art, its active cultivation is our responsibility. How does that lifelong process look when viewed from the perspective of many decades of practice?

Surely the art of ministry calls for a rightful sense of pride in the calling. Taking pride, in the sense of the essential worth of the pastoral calling, means that regardless of who is or isn't noticing and whatever the work at hand might be, it's worth the best we can give to it. It means continually striving for excellence in the varied works of daily ministry. Care for language comes to mind. For years I have regularly read a number of authors of books and magazine articles, not only for enjoyment and mind-expansion but also for study of the art of language found in their writing. I want my sermons to communicate artfully, because the truth of the gospel for today's world deserves and demands care for the language used in communicating the Good News. During the 1960s and 1970s, preaching was denigrated in some areas of the church; social action was all. I have always regarded preaching as a channel for God's Spirit to act, and I didn't give up on it because it was out of fashion. I am grateful for seminary faculty members who held me to the discipline of writing sermons and rewriting them repeatedly until the cliches and flatness and sloppiness were excised and the way was cleared for the Word to work through my words. I am thankful for men and women who have modeled excellence in pastoral ministry for me and, often without their knowing it, have held me to high standards.

Ministry is practiced as an art for the sake of those who receive it. I admire pastors whose ministry allows them to relate to ranchers, street people, racetrack hands, corporate executives, men and women in the armed services, college students, hospital patients, prison inmates, the intellectual elite, and those who never made it through the eighth grade.

And what has been and continues to be the sign to me that grace is coming through in my ministry are those I serve as they meet crisis with courage, receive blessings with gratitude, use their gifts gladly, and, in ways hidden to me but known to God, fight the good fight of faith on lonely fronts in the strength of God's word.

Pastor

When it comes to titles, I have been called Reverend, Rev'ner, Mister, Father, Doctor, and, when I was a student intern in Japan, *Sensei*, which means Teacher. I've probably been called a lot of other things I'm not aware of, and some are best left unmentioned. But the title that is first and best in my mind and heart, the one I love and am most at home with, is "Pastor." It best describes what I do as well as who I am. "Pastor" means shepherd. Christ Jesus is the shepherd, the pastor, who tends the whole flock of God. We can claim that title as those who serve under him, since our calling derives from him. Thus, Pastor Lueking.

From my earliest days, pastors have been splendid shepherds in my life, both in my boyhood and later in my college years. More than they knew, they gave the term a powerful association in my mind without forcing the issue. They influenced me by solid example. When coming to Grace and serving under the senior pastor, Otto Geiseman, I was mentored for a half-dozen years in the rich, full meaning of the term pastor as never before.

I remember a seemingly minor moment on Monday morning, August 16, 1954, my first day on the job after my ordination the previous day. A phone call came through for me as I was getting my new workplace organized. I picked up the receiver and said, for the first time in my life, "Pastor Lueking speaking." That moment, and the impression it made, has stayed with me. It is a privilege beyond words for any human being to be called pastor. The size and scope of this little word, just six letters, still amazes me, and I hope never to lose a proper respect and affection for it.

Pastor is so right as a title because it points beyond the self rather than to it, naming a calling rather than a job title. It's formal but without airs. To me it suggests mutual relationship and yet defines a necessary distance for such relationships to be what God means them to be—if, of course, the one who bears the title of pastor keeps the Chief Shepherd front and center. God gave some to be apostles, prophets, evangelists, *pastors,* and teachers, Paul writes, to equip his people for ministry in his world (Eph. 4:11 ff). *God gave.* Therefore pastors are.

Inevitably, assumptions about pastors emerge over time, and all kinds of images endure as to what pastors should be and do, even how they should look. When I began my pastoral days at Grace, I also began a part-time graduate study program to sharpen my skills for pastoral ministry. I drove my Volkswagen Beetle to and from the University of Chicago campus, and one afternoon I was in too much of a hurry to get back for some duty at Grace. A traffic policeman pulled me over at a spot I can still identify on Chicago's West Side. I rolled down my window and prepared for one of my least-liked activities in life: paying a traffic fine. The cop looked the VW over admiringly (an early model with the turn signals flipping out like lighted wings on either side) and commented: "That little thing'll really fly, won't it!" I nodded meekly. He then looked me over unadmiringly, dressed as I was in a worn plaid shirt, jeans, and an old ball cap on my head. "Anyway, fella, whadd'ya do for a living?" he asked while thumbing through his ticket book for the page I was about to occupy. I paused for effect, drew myself up to full pastoral dignity—not very full, given my outfit, my wheels, and my youthful look—and answered: "I am an ordained Lutheran pastor." He did a sort of double take, took a half-step back, and asked in surprised disbelief: "Full time?" "Yup" was the best I could come up with. He came up with a full-time ticket, after which I drove on to Grace. *Slowly.* Cops are not the only ones who hold stereotypical notions of how we should look and what we should wear. All that is beside the point of who we are in shepherding the people of God.

One of the sure marks that *pastor* is the right title for me has been the ease with which children come to use it. From kindergarten through high school, they use the word readily to get my attention. A favorite and frequent visitor to my study door was eight-year-old Bradford, a child in our parish parochial school. His knock on my door would often come a few minutes before classes began. I would recognize the top of his head, just visible through the colored glass panes in the upper half of the office door, welcome Bradford, and hear his stock question every time: "Well, Pastor, how are things going?" Pastor—not Mister, not Doctor, not Dean—was the right word to give him confidence. The Chief Shepherd knows his sheep; pastor is exactly the right word for me as his under-shepherd, welcoming youngsters at my door and helping them feel at home with what I am called to offer.

My memory returns to a hospital visit with Clara Sievert, who was battling a serious illness at the time. I was just underway with words of scriptural promise and encouragement when a young intern breezed into the room, saw my collar, guessed my purpose, and suggested in an impatient tone that I could do whatever I was there to do—later. This was his turf. He was a busy man, and he let me know it. Clara sat bolt upright in bed, weak though she was, and announced, "This is my pastor"—in a defining tone that made it clear who could wait and who could continue. That was an unusual experience, one of only a handful among thousands of hospital calls in which I have invariably received every courtesy from doctors and nurses who respect their patients as whole persons with souls as well as bodies. Clara's declaration was not spoken in anger or defiance. Rather, I still hear her saying it to establish that she knew what she needed at that moment. Recalling it gives me humility and gratitude for what pastors are given to offer, and for people who know what pastors are for.

In my view the full weight of the term pastor comes when standing with a spouse, parent, child, or family as the casket is closed over someone long loved and sorely missed. Or when a marriage has died, a spouse has become an ex-spouse, and yet a pastor is still there for support. Or in the happy pastoral work of preparing couples for marriage, receiving their trust, being allowed entrance into their deeper lives as they come for preparatory sessions, and then standing with them at the altar on their great day. Or when participating in some humdrum committee meeting and discovering ways to help parishioners wade through the routines toward outcomes that are hardly humdrum. Or when enjoying the unique experience of what some refer to as the afterglow following a well-preached text. I've wondered about that term "afterglow," for it suggests lit cigars to me, but I have no better substitute for the privilege of preaching. There is also an opposite sensation pastors know, this pastor included: it's knowing that we have bombed in the pulpit.

In all of these and countless other moments, pastor is an uncommonly treasured word because of all it signifies. I wouldn't prefer another title, be it president, governor, captain, pope, bishop, chief, honored sir, right reverend, head honcho, or whatever. Somebody has to be the things these titles imply, as they have importance, of course. But Pastor Lueking: that's who I am and what I do. That's the best word, because it is the best fit.

Vocation

The average American, we are told, can expect to make seven job changes in the course of a working lifetime. I've seen signs of that eye-opening statistic and its effects upon Grace members through the years. I have also contrasted it with my dinosaur status of having only one job, *one job in one place,* for 44 years. More and more women entering the ranks of the salaried workforce increase the pace of job change because they are too often the last hired and first fired. Furthermore, the dramatic drop-off of those working small farms since the end of World War II as a result of the agribusiness takeover of the farming industry has meant that millions of farmers now do something else for a living. When I entered ministry, I could find any number of shops nearby selling typewriters; I wouldn't know where to look even for a typewriter ribbon today. Openings for telephone operators were once commonplace entries in newspaper classified ads; in this computer age one calls for tech assistance and talks to India or South Africa. One meets motel proprietors from Pakistan when signing in at a Motel 6, or works side by side with Hispanics at the local market. Somebody used to make clamp-on roller skates, hula hoops, horse collars, and Studebakers. Those somebodies, or their children, now work as computer nerds explaining Ethernet functions to computer klutzes like me, or as employees serving up fast food in chain restaurants, or as salespeople negotiating new markets in Asia. The world of work, now vexed with globalization issues that widen the gap between the industrial and the developing countries, is topsy-turvy as never before.

We're not the first or last generation to experience mercurial change in the ways of making a living in a world that never stands still. All the more reason, then, for one of the rarest treasures of our faith tradition to be recognized and made central to the daily mission of the people of God in the world. The key word is *vocation*.

The Latin root, *vocare*, means "to call." Vocation begins when God calls people into the fellowship of his Son through baptism. It is this call, Martin Luther said, that every baptized person is to renew every morning as the sign of the cross is made, the Holy Trinity invoked, and a hymn sung. Whether that is the manner in which we mark the founding call of God to faith is not the point. What does matter is that baptism is revered in the church and its gospel promise claimed as the power for lifelong discipleship. Vocation, based in baptism, is lived out in the major spheres of life (family, marriage, parenthood, the single life, and the work one does), and becomes a specific calling, lived out according to the particular gifts that God provides. These specific callings give purpose, meaning, and fulfillment to these fundamental areas of life that are constantly threatened by the idolatries of greed, consumerism, and individualism that course through our popular culture. Life has meaning in doing what one does because of what Christ has first done for us. Rather than self-glory, the glory of God is its end. It is not in individualism but in the community of faith that motives for serving in the church and world are formed and sustained. Living the vocation of being a parent or student or worker on the job makes a difference that can be visible to others who are drawn to what they see. Then doors can open for the most vital form of witness, when testimony to the lordship of Jesus Christ comes as an answer to a question: "What makes you different?" Evangelism is not canned advertising for a religious brand, but offering the gospel in word and deed to another who wants to be a part of an authentic, powerful, winsome, and welcoming community.

Vocation gives work meaning. It is partnership with the Creator in his ongoing work of creation for the wider good in the world. When vocation is viewed in this way, the daily job is a different experience. Although it is inevitably laborious, work is blessed. It satisfies when pursued as vocation. Meaning, satisfaction, and fulfillment endure despite any number of job changes, losses, and recoveries during a lifetime. Who does not covet such a treasure for that which takes up the greater share of our waking hours?

Martin Luther developed this theme famously in his view that the peasant farmer plowing, the housewife scrubbing floors, and the merchant about his business in the town were Christ's people whose vocation was in no way inferior to that of priests, bishops, and popes. The framework for Luther's powerful emphasis upon the sacredness of vocation in one's daily work came from the gospel itself. Christ's work of atonement for sin removed forever the need to seek God's acceptance through works, particularly the work of the priesthood. Now that Christ has come, the priesthood belongs to all believers, as 1 Peter 2:9 teaches: "But you are a chosen race, a royal priesthood, a holy nation, God's own people, in order that you may proclaim the mighty acts of him who called you out of darkness into his marvelous light." In this priestly *vocation* bestowed through baptism, each serves the other for the common good. Housewife, farmer, and merchant glorify God where God intends his glory to shine: in the daily life of the world where his mighty acts bring light from darkness, order from chaos, and meaning from futility.

Seeing daily work as a vocation delivers one from one of the most pervasive ills of our time, establishing one's entire identity around work. If the job is my all, then I am nothing when it goes. If the job is really all about salary and benefits, plus the prestige factor, the setup for workaholism is in place. Conversely, if the job is sought for its cushy absence of any challenge, then the stage is set for giving the least rather than the best, ennui is ever at hand, and the growth that comes through a lively sense of vocation is sidelined.

Vocation, relevant to everybody, all the time, is learned in the community of faith. If I could start pastoral ministry all over again, I would attempt to implant its meaning far more intentionally through preaching, teaching, visiting people at work, and every other means at hand. Since I can't do that, but only advocate it, I can nevertheless speak of Grace Church's exemplars of vocation with admiration and gratitude for their witness. Those briefly described here represent many more, impossible to name, who honor God and bless the world as a daily leaven in their work.

Sophie Barradas, a Mexican immigrant and single mother of three, built her own business making high-quality hairpieces (the one she gave me as a surprise I have yet to work up nerve enough to wear). And while her English is not eloquent, she is present for worship regularly and is happiest when she is part of the church kitchen crew preparing food for others. Martin Baumgaertner is a federal judge whose integrity deserves wider press amidst all the politicized babble about activist judges who bend the law out of shape. Margaret Kruse has been a teacher of fifth-grade children for years, her chief vocational satisfaction coming from helping children taste the excitement of learning as a lifelong vocation. Wayne Schroeder, now at rest in Christ, not only sold paint but also helped his company flourish, held the respect of colleagues and customers, and did not withhold the witness to faith when the timing was right. Bob Peterson is a Chicago police officer who is trusted by vulnerable people on his beat who have not found it easy or obvious to trust the person behind the badge. David Hoyem, a certified public accountant whose accounting skills and droll Norwegian humor enrich a prominent Chicago firm, has blessed Grace Church for years as treasurer. Bob Hale has weathered the ups and downs of the commercial radio and television world with his integrity intact, a lifetime of Sunday worship providing the foundation for his weekday steadiness in the slippery media world.

Marilyn Heimburger—a wife, mother, homemaker, and bookkeeper/office manager—is partner with her husband in the unique calling of publishing books on the history of American railroads. Milton Tatter, God rest his soul, was the plumber everybody wanted, ready at any hour for almost any job—including many hours in the boiler room of Grace Church. Kathi Bein took her skills of teaching English as a second language from classrooms of the Chicago Public School to six fruitful years in the Lutheran kindergarten of Ofuna, Japan. Doris Christopher founded her own company of fine cookware in her basement more than 20 years ago and is now president and CEO of an international firm that employs more than 70,000 people who keep faith with the Pampered Chef's mission to gather the family together for meals in a time when that is no longer the norm.

Matthew Ewert, a high-school student, rounded up 90 bicycles for repair and shipped them to South America for use in families where a bike is a lifeline to work and a step up from poverty. Bob Carlson is the comptroller of a company in which he serves with excellence and in addition has made time for board membership on a foundation providing education programs for inmates of the Cook County Jail. Mary Olson, an at-home mother during her own son and daughter's growing-up years, has been foster mother to more than 60 infants and toddlers while each awaited permanent adoption. Bruce Van Heukelem is a partner with Case Hoogendoorn, a Chicago law firm with a high reputation for moral integrity and legal expertise; together with other colleagues they host downtown Chicago breakfast meetings around Scriptures that connect Word and work. Marge Houck, now nearing age 100, has offered a lifetime of generous philanthropic support for various community and church causes and is a model for a new generation that needs to learn how to make affluence count for the public good as well as in support of the church's mission.

Bill Scarlett played trumpet in the Chicago Symphony for years and graced many a Grace Church cantata and concert throughout that time. David Moeller can document the rise and fall of jobs in his own computer career; his anchor in the life of the congregation has seen him through the best and worst of times. Rosemary Lipka fills the term "secretary" with the dignity, grace, and fundamental meaning of calling through her remarkable years of administrative service, including her time at Grace Church. Jeff Cribbs, a financial consultant, promotes sound stewardship as well as prudent money management; he also makes room in his schedule to donate time and talent to mentally handicapped people struggling to live more independently.

Mel Holli writes and teaches as a university professor of urban history, focusing on Chicago's unique historical blend of politics, industry, and immigrant life in one of America's true melting-pot cities. Linda Bernard, a nurse educator, brings the art of patient care into focus along with her medical expertise. Dennis Forgue is a numismatist who travels the world in search of rare coins, but his place in the first row on Sundays at Grace Church is rarely empty. Rich Schupkegel, a computer analyst and programmer, translates the vagaries of this exploding industry into usable systems for schools and businesses. David Heinz's talent as a furniture designer and artist-craftsman who works with wood defies the generalization that there are no more geniuses in this calling; the Grace communion table and our splendid altar carvings are his witness. Ayisha McMillan is a graceful ballerina, well on her pioneering way as an African American in the fiercely competitive field of professional ballet.

These and countless others like them are embodiments of *vocation,* doing what they do because of what Christ Jesus has first done for them. Their talents are wonderfully varied. They know the tediousness as well as the satisfactions of the daily round. Their work is not the center of their life; each lives in a wide web of significant relationships in family, friendships, and congregation. Above all, they live in the grace of God, whose Son redeemed them and whose Spirit works in their lives to make their daily work an offering to him and a service to others. This grace is the source of their job satisfaction as well as their guard against idolizing it. As I have known them and caught at least something of their vocation as Christians, the word *vocation* is less and less an abstraction. These and all the others they symbolize are part of the glue whereby God holds the world together.

In their various ways, each is an expression of the art of ministry, the ministry of the people of God at work in home and workplace, congregation and community. They are also living signs of the grace of the pastoral ministry given to me and other pastoral colleagues who preceded and follow me at Grace Church. Serving them, worshiping with them, preaching and teaching to and with them, and visiting them in their homes and daily places of vocation are great blessings to me, but more than that. They and many more with them personify the purpose for which God gave me my pastoral vocation—to equip them for their daily ministry in the world, that together with all his people we too might "come to the unity of the faith and of the knowledge of the Son of God, to maturity, to the measure of the full stature of Christ" (Eph. 4:11–13).

2

〜

The Virtues of Ministry

EFORE COMMENTING ON A CLUSTER OF VIRTUES NEEDED
in pastoral ministry, it's worthwhile pausing to think
about virtue as a word with an interesting past. Virtue, which the ancient Greeks called *arete*—excellence and
valor—has enjoyed a long and distinguished career in human
thought. Homer regarded it as a nobility in humans derived
from the gods. The classic Greek philosophers saw it as decency
and good order. Aristotle wrote of virtue in his *Nichomachean
Ethics* as a quality of life composed of prudence, justice, tem-
perance, and fortitude. The Cappadocian fathers of Eastern
Christendom—St. Basil and St. Gregory of Nyssa—used the
classical Greek idea of virtue as moderation as a forerunner to
the Christian ideal of virtue as an imitation of the trinitarian life
of God in all its fullness. The Western Christian tradition, led by
Augustine, added the three Pauline or "theological" virtues of
faith, hope, and charity to the classical list, and amplified it by
frequent references to Philippians 4:8, in which St. Paul cites
things true, honest, just, pure, lovely, and of good report as
essential to the *arete* Christians are called to ponder and emulate. For Luther, the heart of virtue is the forgiveness of sins,
lived out by those who are free from the demands of the law
and yet willingly beholden to serve the neighbor in love. Calvin
saw virtue as the righteous life gained in Christ and essential
to citizenship in the earthly commonwealth that reflects the
heavenly kingdom. Dietrich Bonhoeffer was martyred by the
Nazis in 1945 before he could fully develop a treatise on ethics that is suggested in his *Life Together,* a poignant description
of virtue as intimate communion with Christ through prayer,

community, mutual confession, and absolution. More recently the American moralist William Bennett wrote a thick volume, a bit presumptuously titled *The Book of Virtues,* in which he sought to define virtue through hundreds of anecdotal stories aimed against a downward societal slide into moral chaos.

The point of mentioning these references is to suggest that virtue is not an abstract ideal but is related to a way of life variously envisioned in differing times. What I set forth in this chapter is a cluster of virtues at the core of the pastoral life that are rooted in the divine Word made flesh, Jesus Christ. I've heard such pastoral *arete* summed up simply as "doing your best in whatever you do because of what Christ has first done for you." That's not a bad definition at all, especially when seen as motivation that permeates all that pastors do as Christ's servants.

Accountability

"Just who is your boss, anyway?" is a question I've been asked occasionally over the years. It's not one to bristle over defensively. Answering it honestly after thinking carefully about it helps build pastoral accountability.

It's not always obvious to whom we are accountable. I'm not alone in the fact that as a pastor I start and end my workday, choose priorities, deploy energies, use money, produce results, envision challenges, and work out my commitments to family and friends without the daily scrutiny of an overseer. Although I have always worked as part of a church staff, my situation is not so different from the majority of clergy who do not. We clergy have systems of accountability that vary widely, but the truth of the matter is that the pastor can be either the hardest-working person in town or the biggest slacker.

The obligation to hold clergy accountable can suffer because of an aura of holiness placed around the pastor by others (or by pastoral self-promotion), making some people hesitate to ask hard questions of us and our accountability. I can't recall that being an issue at Grace, but perhaps there have been times and circumstances when I should have been asked to give an account of myself in a direct manner. Lutherans have a long tradition of high regard for the *Herr Pastor* image, which can be dangerous when used as a buffer against accountability. I don't think we are alone in this regard.

Through the years I always worked with what my tradition calls "elders," men and women elected to oversee the spiritual life of the congregation, with whom I met and to whom I reported each month. In an organizational sense, these leaders were my boss. In the first half of my pastoral years, the elders consisted of three men; over the second 22 years, the board was expanded to nine and, happily, included women. After my first years of ministry I began to prepare a written outline for the elders of what I was thinking and doing. The more I did it, the more I learned to turn it into something more than selective success stories. I was free to speak about where I came up short or missed altogether, as well as where I knew that solid work was going on. This approach built trust between the elders and me. I could not fool them and had no reason to try.

Another built-in accountability arrangement was the monthly meeting with the church council, made up of representatives from the key areas of parish life—our name for what other traditions call the board or vestry or session. I chaired those meetings for years and had to account for agendas and outcomes. Later on, the council was chaired by the president of the congregation, an improvement in many ways. At the annual meeting of the congregation, my pastoral report was one among others presented to the congregation. Such were the arrangements, quite visible and appropriate, for people not only to know what I was doing but to hold me accountable in ways healthy for all of us. Yet as necessary as these provisions are, they do not really get to the heart of accountability.

Accountability is an outward expression of an inward quality of integrity. Such accountability arises from faith, the conviction that I am—like every other Christian—accountable to God. I might be able to fool others for a time, but God is to be feared and can never be fooled. Yet even our understanding that we are accountable to God can subtly become an abstraction. Something tangible is still needed to mediate accountability. For me it is the congregation.

The late Lutheran theologian and gifted preacher Joseph Sittler recalled a moment during his parish ministry days when, as he greeted people at the church door after the service, one prescient woman said (regarding his hastily thrown-together sermon): "I gather you've been very busy this week." He got the message. A moment of accountability was at hand, and he knew he could not dodge it.

I can remember Shirley Krier's greeting me with "Where'n hell have you been?" It had been too long since I had made the trip to the charity hospital where she was cared for in loneliness with multiple sclerosis, mobile only in a wheelchair, abandoned by her spouse and family. The congregation at Grace was all she had, and with her tart opening words, she let me know that I had flunked the test of coming with the frequency that she needed and deserved. Week after week, I looked out from the pulpit into the faces of men, women, and children whom I loved and served. They were my continuing reminder of my account-ability to God, who called me to them. Often I sat with people in every imaginable dilemma of faith and life; I was accountable to each one in providing pastoral counsel that was a faithful witness to God's judgment, wisdom, and above all, consoling mercy. At the bedsides of people, whether ill with curable or terminal disease, I was accountable to the Great Physician in all those visits. In meetings of every kind, routine and crucial, as I exercised pastoral leadership I was accountable to God in the presence of his people, and I will one day be required to give a final accounting of my stewardship. Then I shall know in full what it means to live by grace, not by works.

Accountability in the daily practice of ministry cannot be precisely measured, but that does not mean that it can be avoided or resented. What produces it and sustains it is "the love of Christ [that] constraineth us" (2 Cor. 5:14 KVJ). Any accountability that stops with human systems can be manipulated. But not the inward sort. It comes from God, and in my experience of it, is offered back to God *through* the myriad ways of serving.

Authority

"I am a fourth-generation Lutheran," he began his speech, this man who added tension to an already tense congregation meeting. I knew that this beginning signaled trouble, the kind that comes from an appeal to authority based on longevity in a denomination.

On another occasion in a different setting I recall a pastor warning us that "I have 16 points to my presentation." He handed down this discouraging news in a pulpit tone of terminal annoyance. Here he sought authority from the sheer number of points in his outline, propped up by the accoutrements of clerical garb and an absolutely ponderous pectoral cross that could bring on curvature of the spine. I gathered that the intention was to overwhelm all present. I was underwhelmed.

Pastors have power—more than we realize. It's folly to play dumb to it. Whether he's aware of it or not, whether it's used or misused, the pastor has power.

Authority is distinguished from power. Authority is given; power is claimed. Authority is earned; power is imposed. Authority comes from power responsibly used, including the power to disavow the popular assumptions about power—as did Jesus in his Sermon on the Mount, or Gandhi in his teaching on the power of passive resistance, or Martin Luther King, Jr., with his commitment to nonviolence as the greatest power of all. Authority is the rare, virtuous result of the long, careful building up of people, of keeping power in its place, free from domination, free for persuasion. Authority has an appealing, beckoning quality. At our best, we humans know we can't have a livable community without it. Authority is God-given.

For us Christians it is embodied in our crucified Savior, whose authority came through the giving of his life for all of us, even to the last and the least.

I became aware of this distinction between authority and power especially during the decade of the 1960s, a time of craziness in America. Student activists trashed campus buildings. Demonstrators torched cities across the land and staged sit-ins against war and racial injustice. Proponents of the sexual revolution advocated sleeping together with no thought of marriage. Opting out of the establishment was the thing to do for a brave new generation, with little thought given to what doing so meant. Much of this defiance of authority was the tragic outcome of raw power used by those in authority to quash legitimate protest against the abuses of injustice and the madness of war. The irony was that those who adopted the label of the Moral Majority in the 1960s and 1970s, exercising raw power to impose law and order, lost the authority to prevail; the resignation of Richard Nixon from the presidency in 1974 and the loss of the Vietnam War were painful evidence for the whole nation to experience.

Against the tumult of those events, aspects of which carried over into an ugly battle brewing in our denomination, the Lutheran Church–Missouri Synod, I found it necessary to face matters of misused power and necessary authority emerging in our congregation. (I had become senior pastor at Grace in 1963, after nine years of serving as assistant and then associate pastor in the congregation.) Wobbly and tentative though my efforts were as a young pastor, they were an expression of the authority that comes from simply following Jesus—which is never all that simple. When Chicago's West Side was going up in flames of violence, I invited all at Grace—all who were ready—to join in inter-parish Bible study groups, each made up of black and white Lutherans from Chicago congregations and our own, that would meet regularly at various group members' homes and be led by hosts from each congregation. I recall well one elder's question when I proposed the idea. "You mean black people will be walking up the sidewalk to our door in our all-white neighborhood?" Yes was the answer, based on the authority written all over the New Testament's message of reconciliation among alienated people. And it happened. Not with everyone from Grace or its partner black congregations. But those who were ready to participate did so in response to an authority thoroughly traceable to the Christ whose reconciling love works through fallible mortals.

The Vietnam War years, and to a lesser extent the 1990s, when the first U.S. war with Iraq took place, were times of tough choices for young men and their families. They are with us now as the current quagmire of a war in Iraq continues, as issues of sexual ethics threaten to split Christian churches worldwide, and as illegal immigration and the predicament of illegal immigrants pose issues that must be faced. As our red state/blue state political impasse persists on so many hot-button issues, the need grows for the congregation to be the setting for thorough, probing moral discourse informed by biblical faith. In such a setting, pastoral authority does not mean telling each one what to do but keeping the Word hearable and doable despite all the ruckus and complexity that build on all sides.

In exercising pastoral authority, one does not have to coerce and cajole. Instead, the best tack is to embody the law and the gospel in preaching and deed, seeking to combine courage with humility where each is needed—as indeed they are always when one is ministering to people with sharply differing views. Looking back, I believe that during the most tumultuous times, I became the pastor of the congregation at a deeper level than when ordained. Yes, I was called to preach the Word, administer the sacraments, and tend to the flock of God. But like all other clergy, I had to grow into pastoral authority, sometimes boldly, sometimes not; I was sometimes well received as pastoral leader, sometimes not; often energized by pastoral colleagues, sometimes having to stand and deliver alone.

As much as I love the beauty of worship, especially the thrilling music given us by music director Paul Bouman in those years, and as much as I enjoyed the increased use of vestments— colorful and historic as they are—I grew in the awareness that authority is not about what one wears while leading worship. Authority is what comes from my heart and head and hands, used as they were by the Lord Christ. I would have been just as authoritative leading worship in street clothes, as did Augustine all through his 30 years as the bishop of Hippo in the fifth-century church of North Africa. And my high-church friends added a welcome note of humor to the subject with their story about the actress Tallulah Bankhead, who, well mellowed by holiday spirits and attending a Christmas Eve mass, greeted the elaborately vested priest, gravely swinging the incense vessel, with "I love your frock, dahling, but your purse is on fire." The smells and bells do not produce authority, any more than pounding the Bible in shirtsleeves.

Authority can't be dodged, even as it can't be commandeered. It is given, and it must be used forthrightly. It is basic to the exercise of the pastoral office. I grew in the realization that—all the craziness of the times notwithstanding—people need authority and deep down long for it. Humans respond to it instinctively, despite all the baggage we carry as the spiritual offspring of Adam and Eve. We are created in the image of God and for that reason long for God-given authority. As long as everyone, pastors especially, and this pastor in particular, keeps clear that authority is God's gift and not our oyster, authority will continue to bless rather than burden.

On my last Sunday as pastor at Grace, while I was distributing Holy Communion, eight-year-old Audrey, a beautiful child with auburn hair framing her trusting face, put her arms right around my waist and hugged me tight. It caught me so by surprise, her courage and spontaneous love, that tears came to my eyes, and I could not find my voice to speak a blessing on her. So I just hugged her back. It was a kind of ordination, a receiving of authority all over again.

Creative Fidelity

Creative fidelity is a two-word summary of a virtue that belongs in pastoral ministry, indeed one that should be coveted by everybody in every walk of life. In the pastoral calling, *creative* suggests openness to the future, readiness for needed innovation, purposeful change, and effective newness of the sort inspired by God the Holy Spirit. For centuries, after all, the church has prayed *Veni Creator Spiritus*, and we ought to be prepared when the Creator Spirit does create renewing gifts for mind and soul. *Fidelity* speaks of respectful continuity with the past, solid grounding, faithfulness to the lively tradition of the gospel handed down from the prophets and apostles as the core of all Christian belief and life, as Paul puts it in 1 Corinthians 15:3: "For I handed on to you as of first importance what I in turn had received: that Christ died for our sins in accordance with the scriptures, and that he was buried, and that he was raised on the third day in accordance with the scriptures." *Creative* spells hope for the future. *Fidelity* spells faithfulness to our roots.

I keep learning creative fidelity from many sources. My first real theological vision of it came in my first year of seminary, especially under Professor Richard Caemmerer. What was creative was his theological genius in teaching, his gift for making the monosyllables of the faith—death, sin, law, life, love, faith, hope—come alive as I had never experienced them before. His theological method was faithful to the scriptural gospel; he served not only Lutherans but also people in the wider ecumenical tradition of the church. His classes were exciting. I looked forward to them eagerly and talked about them enthusiastically to anybody ready to listen.

Beginning pastoral ministry at Grace under Otto Geiseman helped me see creative fidelity in new ways. He was pastorally creative in preaching, pastoral care, counseling, and administrative vision; yet the grounding for it all was unmistakably the biblical witness to Jesus Christ the Lord. Among other things, he guided Grace through its post-World War I transition from German-language worship to English-language worship, moved the parish from cultural isolation to community outreach, and led the congregation to plan and build a magnificent new sanctuary in the worst of the 1930s Depression years and to pay for it by 1947. Something of his impatience with traditionalism (which theologian Jaroslav Pelikan has called "the dead faith of the living, contrasted with Tradition as the living faith of the dead") comes through in an exasperated comment I once heard Geiseman make to fellow pastors who needed to hear it: "There's nothing wrong with you that reading a new book and getting your pants pressed wouldn't help." I could not have had a finer model of creative fidelity in pastoral ministry.

My first venture into this subject came as the 35-year-old new senior pastor at Grace, soon after my predecessor's untimely death. How to honor his memory? I proposed not a monument in stone but a living endowment to support new ministries that were in need of seed money to get them started. Through the years, Kingdom Frontiers has provided start-up funding for scores of new ministry ventures in and beyond Grace Church. Among the needs for creative and faithful ministry I came across within the congregation was for a setting in which our doctors and nurses could come together for open discussion without threat of litigation, staff conflicts, medical mistakes that could be crippling or fatal to patients, and vexing ethical issues often centered on the beginning and ending of human life. One of our pastoral associates took the lead in organizing these gatherings of members who found Saturday afternoons from three to five the best time to discuss common challenges, share experiences, and welcome the practice of confession and absolution before concluding. All of them reported that there was no place other than the congregation for such sharing. Not long after that group started, lawyers and business people were invited to organize similar groups within their own disciplines.

It took me a decade to become creatively faithful in improving pastoral ways to prepare youth for confirmation, and those ways included the adding of gifted laymen and laywomen to the confirmation teaching team. Ruth Zeddies was the first woman to be elected elder at Grace in the 1970s, the first of many women to follow in using their gifts in every area of leadership and service in the congregation, including Phyllis Kersten, who arrived in 1996 as our first ordained woman on the pastoral staff.

Adoption of the new *Lutheran Book of Worship* as our hymnal in the late 1970s was a creatively faithful expansion of our worship life, gracefully and skillfully led by music ministers Paul Bouman and Carl Schalk. The 15 years of painful parish involvement in a denominational struggle was a maximum test of pastoral creative fidelity.

Among the most challenging as well as rewarding experiences of creative fidelity given me was in the transition from active pastorate to active retirement, a move mercifully spared the pitfalls and horror stories too often associated with transitions after long-term pastorates.

Two experiences reflect the worst and best of what I have tried to be and do in creatively faithful ministry.

The worst—or better stated, the most bizarre—was applying my own idea of a creative solution to a denominational conflict involving our building and property. The details of the conflict are not important here; what I thought could be done was to resolve the matter by literally moving our entire sanctuary and school complex to a Dominican Priory location some hundred yards or so across the street. I took it upon myself to research the possibility of such a move. The technology was available; buildings in Chicago twice that size had been moved, and I went to look at them. I then met privately with the priory leadership about my plan, learned of its polity that the local community of the order has the authority to sell or retain its property, asked the community of several dozen priests to take my idea seriously by putting it to a vote—all of which happened. Their deliberations on whether to sell a portion of their empty land to us failed by a three-vote margin. Why did I go about this effort without taking the parish leadership and members into my brainstorming? I did so because the conflict engulfing us had become Chicago news and national news during the 1970s, and we were obligated to enter into sensitive and expensive litigation to defend our right to the property. Rather than make public the option of moving the building before I could learn whether it was possible, and before I could lead the congregation through the process of understanding such a prospect, I chose not to expose us to further unwanted publicity and court costs. So I kept the idea to myself. Had the building move been made possible by a green-light vote from our Dominican neighbors, I would, of course, have presented what I thought was a creative solution to the congregation and sought the approval of all necessary parties. It didn't happen (though I still savor the picture of our magnificent neo-gothic structure, jacked up on pneumatic supports, steadied by a network of cables, moving slowly across Division Street!). Why put this exercise in pastoral creativity at the bottom of my list of imaginative ideas? Because it proposed a real-estate solution to what was at heart a theological and ecclesiastical issue. A decade later it was resolved on that basis, and we are the better as a congregation for having taken no shortcuts to reach it.

One of the best affirmations of creative fidelity came through helping to form a national program for continuing education of clergy based on what is learned in the practice of ministry. It all began with an article in *The Christian Century* by pastoral theologian Granger Westberg, a man whose lifelong passion to bridge the gap between theological and medical education kept him constantly thinking ahead of the curve. His subject was "Why Not an Academy of Parish Clergy?," modeled after academies of general practitioners in the medical field. He included me in his invitation to a dozen clergy, Protestant and Roman Catholic, to meet in Houston, Texas, on an Easter Monday. We were all a bit tired, of course, after Holy Week duties. But Granger quickly stirred up our lagging energies with his vision of creating something new and needed. For two days he worked us from early till late; then, as we finished work at the end of the second day, cheered us with the surprise announcement that a generous Houston layman was ready to host us for a steak dinner and a night of baseball at the Astrodome. It turned out to be the longest night game in history, scoreless until an error in the 23rd inning allowed an Astros run to score and brought the game to an end. We stumbled back to our hotel, slept fast, met Granger the next morning, agreed to the formation of the Academy of Parish Clergy, and went home to rest up. Despite the unusual beginnings, I have treasured my ongoing associations with the Academy, giving me opportunity to learn from male and female colleagues from around the country and across the ecumenical spectrum. It is creative; no other program I know of offers a disciplined way for parish clergy to teach each other by sharing what we learn in the daily practice of ministry. It can claim fidelity by honoring the unique theological tradition of each participant without requiring compromise. Roman Catholic, Protestant, and Jewish clergy belong, learn, share, and enjoy growing and helping other grow in the calling.

Creative fidelity takes an endless variety of forms among the third of a million or more clergy in the United States. In my experience, it is one of the most valued gifts we can cultivate. I am indebted to many colleagues for their example, and am grateful to keep sharing my portion of this charism at this stage of my journey.

Ethics

In recent decades the American public has endured or been titillated by all-too-many lamentable accounts of clergy who misused money, sexually exploited parishioners, or pursued power and status to the shame of the profession we all represent. Church bodies have sought to prevent these offenses through better screening of ordination candidates. But the issue of pastoral ethics is never ending, and every one of us does well to begin each day petitioning God to keep our eyes open to how vulnerable *we* are to the calamities celebrated in the juicer headlines.

My seminary education was weak in pastoral ethics. It consisted of cases of possible ministerial predicaments with little or no theological basis. One section of a pastoral manual advised what to do when confronted with the prospect of "baptizing Siamese twins." But the theological foundations given me in other courses during my seminary years of the late 1940s and early 1950s helped me build the ethics of my pastoral practice.

This theological foundation for pastoral ethics is trinitarian, God's creative goodness revealed in the grace of Jesus Christ for the transformation of life in the Holy Spirit. The framework for ethical decision making and action that I drew from this central truth is fairly uncomplicated, growing out of four basic questions: Does my action reflect faithfully upon the lordship of Christ as witnessed in sacred Scripture? Does my action serve the good of others, though it may be personally costly? Do I accept responsibility for the consequences of my actions and seek healing for those I have offended? Does my action sit well in my conscience? I came to these four through listening intently to and watching colleagues in ministry, both lay and ordained.

After ordination, pastoral ethics quickly became a matter of actual rather than academic concern. My ministry of pastoral care began to take shape early in my ministry—largely, I think, because of the potent legacy in pastoral counseling I inherited from my predecessor at Grace, Otto Geiseman. Among the first elements that came home to me as crucial was confidentiality. No one, not even a court of law, can coerce me or any pastor to reveal what is said in the sacred confines of the parishioner's confession and the pastor's absolution—something we do well to appreciate deeply, for that principle is not honored every-where in the world. It awed me, and still does, that people bare their souls—their woes, failures, sins, or shame—to a fellow mortal like me. They invest such trust, consciously or not, not in me but in the One I represent, the Christ who never breaks the trust extended to him in repentance. If we break the trust of others, the ministry of counseling, at least with a person betrayed, suffers a major setback.

There are lessons on this matter to be learned from church history. An example comes from the fateful struggle through which Augustine led the fifth-century church in North Africa. The Donatists against whom he contended declared that clergy who had betrayed the faith under persecution were forever unfit for ministry of any kind and ought not be restored. But Augus-tine held to the deeper truth held that the validity of the Word is not destroyed by the fallibility of the Word-bringer. Its validity rests in God. That's still true, since we clergy, like all other Christians, live by the forgiveness of our sins. But confession is not license for clergy to be careless in talking with anyone about what has been confided in the sanctity of pastoral counseling. I learned to guard that trust as I guard my own life.

A different ethical challenge to me came when I had to admonish someone. I dislike confrontation. It's hard for me to do, but to dodge it is unethical because it permits bad behavior to go unchecked. I recall having to arbitrate among parishioners in conflict and coming to moments when I needed to say: "You are wrong and must come to terms with the damage you are doing." I recall a daylong session with two brothers, one of whom was trying to buy out the other's share in the business they had successfully built for years. It was agony for all three of us. But they finally came to agreement after hours of effort that would not have succeeded without timely moments of my intervening with straightforward admonition. Being good Italians, they finally embraced each other—and me—with hugs and tears.

"A friend is one who warns you," a Jewish proverb says. Telling the truth when it was hard to hear caused sharp reactions at times. I remember an angry man telling me to go straight to hell and stomping out of my study. But to have been simply nice rather than faithful would have meant avoiding the hard work of exposing the sin that was poisoning this parishioner's marriage. Those moments remind me that the pastorate is not a popularity contest. The temptation is to sin by omission, simply to get too busy to meet with people in their most cantankerous, most volatile, least likable moments, or to hand them off to professional counselors, for whom sin and grace might not play an essential part in the process toward healing.

An occasion comes to mind when a fine man called me from the airport, asking if he could come to my study immediately. The first thing he did when sitting down with me was to put his head in his hands and weep. After he had poured out the tears, he told me of the past several days in his life. He had gone out of town on a business trip. While far from home, he received a phone call that took him by surprise. A power play by adversaries within his corporation had cost him his job. He was fired, then and there, over the telephone. While he was trying to absorb the impact of this ugly surprise, a high-class hooker sized him up in the hotel dining room as though she had radar. They ended up in bed. This incident lay even heavier upon him than the company coup. After pouring out his remorse and receiving the absolution of Christ, he asked a question that pushed pastoral ethics to another level: should he tell his wife what had happened? I responded that the decision had to be his. I assured him that Christ's forgiveness restored his relationship to God unconditionally. He was fully known, fully accepted. Telling his wife was not essential to validate that acceptance. If telling her would bind them closer together, it could be ethical to do so, but only if doing so would benefit her and strengthen the marriage. I do not know what action he took, but I am confident that he did what was best for their future together, since they lived on till the end of their days with blessing. I am glad that pastors do not need to check up later in such matters, but only to commend people to God, whose grace is sufficient to carry them through.

A congregation-denomination conflict arose unexpectedly as an unwelcome turn of events at the midpoint of my Grace Church years; and as it developed, it became clear that a court settlement of the property issue was unavoidable. We knew the admonition of Paul in 1 Corinthians 6 that Christians settle matters themselves and do not haul each other into court. Indeed, we did seek every means we knew to keep the question of rightful ownership of our church property out of civil court. We failed. The dispute was a legal issue about the terms of the land contract drawn up in 1927 when Grace bought the property from the neighboring, denominationally owned Concordia College, to build our church and school. The people of Grace had paid for the land in full. After eight years of painful litigation, the matter was finally settled by the U.S. Supreme Court. Without the protection of the First Amendment of the United States Constitution, we would not have kept our property and church building. Here was a legal case in which the civil court provided a system of justice that the church did not.

Issues of pastoral ethics arise most frequently, however, not in protracted litigation but in more commonplace matters of pastoral life that test the essential quality of pastoral integrity. For me they turned up frequently, for example, in talking with people who expressed an interest in transferring to Grace from weak congregations that were growing weaker. I could not claim 20/20 vision in discerning their motives, and it always bothered me to receive members from dying parishes. In other circumstances, when people held only scorn for their present congregation or pastor and made that the reason to transfer, I knew it would not be long before Grace and Lueking were the latest villains. When, in turn, Grace parishioners let me know that Grace was not for them, if indeed they gave me the courtesy of expressing their views, the ethical task was to help them sort out the substantial from the superficial. More often than not, they departed with our blessing, since we are not the only corner in the Lord's vineyard. Integrity in congregational membership becomes an issue of pastoral ethics that will only grow more acute as American Christians do more and more church shopping, influenced by the consumer culture that has come to dominate even the process of seeking a church home. My heart is especially with pastors who lose members to churches that resemble ecclesiastical Wal-Marts choking off surrounding small businesses. Integrity is essential to withstand the strong pull on clergy to add numbers with eyes closed to what is essentially sheep stealing.

Somewhere in his writings, gifted theologian and ethicist George Forell summed up the essence of ethics for Christians in words to this effect: "Do your faithful best, and after you've done it, pray for the forgiveness of sins." That holds true for every Christian, pastors included.

Honesty

Honesty is not separate from ethics, but it shows in specific acts of pastoral practice over which ethics is the broader heading. The ordination vow, in my case as a Lutheran, includes the promise to "adorn the Gospel with a holy life." In making that promise, I learned through the years of its call for honesty in ways I could not appreciate as my ministry began.

Honesty in preaching, of course, means avoiding lies in the pulpit—or anywhere else in pastoral discourse. Striving for eloquence at the expense of clarity poses a particular test of that honesty. Paul spoke of it as those "lofty . . . plausible words of wisdom" (1 Cor. 2:1, 4) that puff up the speaker with vanity rather than build up the listener in love. They are dishonest in that they attempt to make the one speaking other than who he or she really is. The preachers I admire for their gift of clear, graceful, persuasive preaching continue to work at their gift, honing, revising, paring, and improving language so that the Word "may have free course and be preached to the joy and edifying of Christ's holy people" (from the Collect for the Word, *Lutheran Book of Worship*, Morning Prayer, p. 137). The irony is that hearers quickly sort out what is genuinely the preacher's work and what is someone else's. Woe to preachers who think otherwise! But those who preach and write with disciplined skill endure. I was blessed with wordsmiths among my seminary mentors whose gift made their speech clear rather than cluttered. I still benefit from the discipline of honest preaching that I learned from them.

Plagiarism is another blight on honesty in preaching and pastoral ministry in general. Why do we steal from others and call their work our own? Because of the "I wish I had said that" syndrome? Our own insecurity? Or pride? Or laziness? Perhaps the most benign explanation is mismanagement of time. The temptation to help ourselves to another's solid work is strong when Sunday is coming and it's already Friday afternoon. I know from experience. For years I have published a sermon series intended to prime the pump of preacher subscribers. When I have been pushed to the limit to meet a mailing deadline, I have known how strong the pull is to use another's insight or phrase without attribution; may the Lord forgive me for being a slow learner. Yet, I cannot ever recall anyone's complaining because I acknowledged a source quoted.

I have known the pressure to adjust the truth in conflicted situations. A moment comes back to me from an earlier time. It was a tense meeting at Grace with Fellowship Hall packed to the doors. I had established a fund through our parish treasury to receive contributions for the support of colleagues unjustly ousted in a denominational controversy. While I had received the approval of the church council, the general membership did not know of it. A hostile questioner did learn of the fund and sought to nail me publicly by asking whether I had sought the permission of the congregation, which normally has the final word on parish matters. I gave the technically correct answer that the proper leaders had approved. When he pressed me to explain why I had not taken the matter to the congregation at large and told everybody what was going on, I fumbled around with a dissembling comment. Another member arose on the spot and asked the entire assembly for its voice in the matter. The response was overwhelming support. Why didn't I choose to be fully honest from the start? Fear, I suppose. But I learned an important lesson that evening—that being transparently honest to the point of vulnerability is strength, not weakness. If I'm right, I have nothing to hide. If I'm wrong, it's neither illegal, immoral, nor fattening to say so publicly and let all gain by the experience.

Pastoral honesty in handling money hardly needs extended comment. I'm glad I had no part in handling parish money, and only once in all my years did I need to confront a member who had pocketed some offerings himself. When I traveled on church business, receipts were required from me as well as from anyone else. Scrupulous honesty in submitting such documentation has been a safeguard against even the appearance of wrongdoing, and never a drag. There has been and always will be quite enough public scandal swirling around clergy mismanagement of money. There's no need to add fuel to that fire.

Probably the most common testing of honesty comes in reporting pastoral performance. Like many congregations, Grace Church has an annual meeting with written reports from all staff members and officers. The usual run of statistics on pastoral acts, overall trends, and highlight events dominates the report. It may be too strong to characterize these statistics as a wry colleague once described college-catalogue course descriptions, as "light fiction." But total honesty is no doubt more than people can bear or want, since complete candor would blow everybody out of the room—which might be more refreshing than bringing yawns. In any case, I do not recall reporting honestly about calls *not made*, homebound people *neglected*, major challenges *circumvented*, grieving parishioners *never recognized*, disillusioned youth *never sought out*, and wider agonies of the human condition *never prayed for*.

That is why the last word in publicly reporting on pastoral ministry, as well as all ministry by all the baptized, needs to be an appeal for mercy from God, who knows our hearts. The gospel is the only real hope for the honesty that exalts God in the church and dares to tell the whole truth among her servants, this one in particular.

Integrity

"Here I stand..." Luther's famed words, associated with his courageous stand against the pope at the Imperial Diet of Worms, were lettered in bold, old-style German script across the center of a framed "parchment" once passed around during a contentious church convention. In parentheses at the bottom, these words had been added in smaller print, as a rebuke of a theologically compromised leader: "I could also stand elsewhere..."

The punch line in parentheses turned Luther's celebrated declaration into a wry comment on the flight from integrity at the most painful denominational meeting of my life. At first glance, the mock document made me smile. On second thought, it made me want to weep. I did so in that denominational convention when the majority of delegates bought into the shameless power game that declared an entire faculty of seminary professors, each a man of integrity, guilty of false doctrine, unfit for the church of God—and then threw them out. When integrity departs, the loss is great. When integrity departs from an assembly gathered under the trinitarian name of God, the actions can turn blasphemous.

Pastoral integrity is the responsibility of every ordained person. But when church leaders charge that faithful pastors are unfit for the church of God because they challenge cheap politicizing, the damage is deep and long-term, especially as it hurts laity who lack ways of seeing what is really going on. Such an assault on pastoral integrity early in my ministry made me aware of the fact that in its still-sinful side, the church can devour its own servants. I make no claim to perfection, as my wife well knows. But God be thanked that integrity is not perfection. The virtue of integrity is a quality of character, Spirit-created, and shaped by the grace of Christ so that belief, thought, and speech reflect it. It is marked by genuineness, consistency, and wholehearted commitment, by one's being the same person regardless of who is looking, or when no one is looking. It is absolutely essential in the pastoral calling. In no other line of work does the word *hypocrisy* come to mind more quickly than when clergy are two-faced. The entire Letter of James is one sustained appeal for integrity in every believer.

If integrity is a word that applies to me, it is so by divine grace alone. I find it awkward to speak of my own integrity, unless it be in the spirit of Paul, who devotes a good deal of 2 Corinthians to defending the integrity of his apostolate against accusers, and whose word in Ephesians 4:11–13 provided my guiding theme for all my years—equipping God's people for daily ministry in the world and being steady in exploring the depths of that truth. What I know about my integrity is that it comes by the daily renewal of my baptism. I am a work in progress, far from finished.

Rather than continuing in this vein, however, a better tack is to speak of ways I have been inspired by the integrity of others—among whom is Gus Baehr. He was one of those parishioners whom I came to know and admire soon after ordination. I had heard stories of his revamping the business practices in the position he held as a senior executive in a major American corporation. His predecessor had trashed associates with abandon in his scramble to the top. Clients were invited to company parties of drunken excess. Contracts were granted via the old-boy network in exchange for playing the company game. I learned about these things not from Gus himself but from those who came from around the country to pay tribute to him at his retirement dinner. One after another, they described Baehr's integrity, which brought needed change from the day he took over. No drunken parties but dinners that wives could enjoy. No good-ol'-boy favors, but rewards for merit demonstrated. He called for high standards, because he personified them in business practice. "When you gave us your word, Gus, we didn't need it in writing" seemed to be the theme of every speech that memorable evening. Much of what I heard then stays in my mind these 40 years later in remembering a man for whom Sunday worship (which he rarely missed) carried over into the workplace. He had a no-nonsense bearing about him, yet he did not intimidate. Rather his consistency of character motivated me, and I sought to practice in my vocation the integrity that his colleagues and competitors had seen in him.

Another memory of a parishioner's integrity comes from much different circumstances: a 15-year-old girl sat in my study, her mother alongside. Some weeks earlier, when walking home from school, she had been attacked and raped. Now she had reason to believe she was pregnant. She felt rotten. Her health was fragile at best, as she faced this new and terrible dilemma. Her mother turned to the subject of abortion. The young woman listened to plausible reasons for that choice. When it came her turn to speak, she simply said no. Her decision was consistent with her conviction that taking a nascent life was not the solution to the crime against her life. Her mother sensed the integrity of her daughter's mind on the matter. There was nothing for me to add except the pledge of pastoral support as all in the family faced daunting times ahead. My next contact with the family came a short time later. The young woman was recovering from a miscarriage. Her integrity had been tested by two crises, the assault and its aftermath. I still hold in my memory the impression of that 15-year-old, sitting across from me, calmly showing an integrity far beyond her years, following through on her convictions, even though she was unsure what the price might be.

I can speak of pastoral integrity from another source, my theological formation in my seminary years. What came through to me was a motif for my calling from Ephesians 4:11–13, which describes the pastoral calling: equipping God's people for daily ministry. Through my years at Grace I found that motif sufficient to give me the identity of who I am and what I am called to do: equip the saints at Grace for their ministry in the daily rounds of life. I have matured and grown, but not apart from that guiding, overarching framework for my calling. For me, then, the virtue of integrity means being the same forgiven sinner, the same pastor with the same motive and vision regardless of the theological, ecclesial, political, cultural, and social changes that have constantly churned around me in the five decades since my ordination. That is no small mercy of God to me. I speak of it with humility and gratitude. And, I hope, with integrity.

Patience

The sure mark of an amateur, it is said, is impatience.

That being said, then, the sure mark of maturity in the pastoral calling must be patience—not patience as in clock-watching or a sigh of resignation: this patience is waiting upon God's time, his moment of fulfillment, his purposes brought to fruition. Such patience is a virtue, listed among the fruits of the Holy Spirit named by Paul in his letter to the Galatians (5:22–23).

I find that living into that virtue of patience is a lifelong project that keeps on delivering surprises as well as challenges. Here is a favorite image for it, taken from weddings at Grace. As the processional music begins, the groom enters from a side door and stands at the center of the nave, eagerly looking to the narthex for the bride to swing into view, move down the aisle, and join him at the altar. In over a thousand weddings in the sanctuary at Grace, I have never seen a groom yawn, look at his watch, or tap his fingers on the end of the first pew. Such patience is anything but routine! He knows *she* is coming, that she will soon come into view and walk down the aisle. That knowledge fills his patience with all the joy, eagerness, and expectancy that love creates in that magic moment. Patience, borrowing from that image, is sure and hopeful because *he*, the Christ of God and Savior of our lives, is the One on whom our patience waits.

A look back over decades of pastoral ministry tells me how totally different our hurry-up, get-it-all-now nature is from the patience that waits upon the slow, sure, grace-filled ways of God to reach fulfillment. I was ordained in the mid-1950s, boom times for church attendance in congregations and evangelistic crusades, when planning for continuing church growth and giving was assumed as certain. I mean no disparagement of mass evangelism, ambitious congregational programs, and high stewardship goals. They can indeed be signs of the Spirit's work, but not when they come at the expense of patient waiting upon the mystery of how Christ's reign works in the church and her mission in the world.

Harry Fawley taught me something about patience as a part of faith. He was a Virginian by birth, married to Ada of our congregation. In his gentlemanly southern way he was politely firm in resisting any coercion in matters of his soul. He accepted my invitation to attend one of the first adult instruction classes I gathered. Some 30 or more adults participated in the 10-week series. I expected Harry, and all the others with him, to join Grace Church as a matter of course at its conclusion. He did not. He would attend church occasionally with Ada. He was unfailingly courteous on all occasions of conversation. But it was more than 20 years before Harry Fawley called me one day, ready at last to sit down and review carefully what believing the gospel and accepting its commitments meant. I had not kept

Harry in my thoughts and prayers all those 20 years or more. It was the patient, probing, gently guiding Spirit of God who kept tilling the soil of Harry's heart till the *kairos* time came at last.

Teachers of Grace School have taught me much about patience. Morella Mensing was a legend in her time as first-grade teacher *par excellence,* and one of her favorite quotations from a first grader of hers to a kindergartner coming up was, "Listen real good; Miss Mensing only tells you stuff once!" Hardly. She told, retold, and told yet again countless things that primary teachers have to repeat, with patience born of wisdom and love for children. Susan Calhoun, along with others, continues that tradition of combining patience with excellence. It's hard work, as all teachers know. So often I've seen Susan in her classroom, working with special-needs children well after the class day ended. I have marveled at the stamina such patience requires as seeds of learning, especially reading, are planted but take years to develop fully. Susan continues as a symbol of the patience that all worthy teachers embody, to the lasting good of all of us who test their patience plenty along the way.

Learning patience spans a lifetime, of course, and perhaps my aptitude for patience has been helped along by the low blood pressure the Creator has given me. A steady 120-over-80 reading does not ensure the deeper things of mind and soul that come only with patience, but it helps when patience is tested by the unwelcome and unexpected.

I was among six interns from the seminary who went to Japan for a two-year stay in 1951. The day after we landed in Yokohama, we met the six missionaries who would become our mentors. When the match-ups were being made, I had a positive impression of all but one of the missionaries—who was, of course, the one to whom I was assigned. I remember well staring a long time at the ceiling on the first night in the bedroom of that missionary home where I was to live, asking God if there was some chance that the two-year vicarage could be shortened to two weeks or, better, two days. His response was the far better, no-shortcuts, tough-but-purposeful lesson on patience, learned through getting along with people who are not one's preference.

My pastoral vision has been sharpened through those lessons learned under circumstances I would not have chosen on my own. From the pulpit, Sunday after Sunday for years, I would look into the faces of people whose patience was tested far more than mine. Patience in chronic illness. Patience in households where faith was not shared by others in the family. Patience in seasons of joblessness or work frustrations. Patience in waiting for friends to understand. Patience in waiting upon prayer to be answered. Patience in finding the desired partner in life. Patience in coming to terms with being single. Patience with self. Patience in waiting for death to come at last. People endure in all of these and countless more life situations, young and old alike. How can I even begin to see and minister to them in their patience unless I have come to know something of the staying power of patience myself? The congregation has been the learning place for patience, and I know I am not alone as I listen to other clergy speak from their experience.

And then there is something to be said for impatience in pastoral ministry, a holy impatience. It turns up all through Jesus's public ministry, especially in Mark's Gospel with its frequently used adverb *immediately* to underscore Jesus's relentless pressing on to the cross and the resurrection beyond. Drawing that quality of holy impatience into pastoral ministry delivers it, I find, from dawdling, as if we had forever to battle the dark principalities and powers. My own experience of holy impatience was most acute during the decade and a half from 1970 to 1985, when parish and denomination collided. I had sometimes to hit the accelerator to bring the congregation to an awareness of the creeping paralysis of legalism; at other times I had to apply the brakes against our simply wanting to get out of the mess. The elders and church council were key partners in finding the right combination of patience and holy impatience, and it would have been folly to have led without their critical counsel and wholehearted support. Much was at stake, involving not only church property but also the health and vigor of our gospel ministry and mission. We did not bat a thousand through those 15 years, but we came through a stronger parish, and I a more patient pastor.

Patience and the wisdom it yields will be needed in all things as Grace, as a part of the church universal, charts its course into the future. Twenty-five or 50 years from now, how will Grace Church best express what it means to be *evangelically catholic,* no oxymoron but a faithful phrase for effective engagement of our confessional tradition with wider membership in Christ's Body, his church? Who will be there to guide? Who to follow? That is not yet clear. But answers there will be. As prayers for the Spirit's gift of patience and wisdom keep on rising from every heart, the patience that waits for God's will to be done in God's time will be given.

Excellence

Settling for second best in matters of pastoral ministry and congregational life, a malady more common than we like to recognize, ranks high among the sins of respectable people. Striving for excellence is an antidote to that spiritual blight. Living out the grace of Christ by loving God, self, and neighbor with the whole heart and mind fosters high standards in the congregation and helps make excellence a way of life. It gives people the genuine lift of being part of a faith community in which all help each other function at their best.

I have a symbol for that excellence. I noticed it early on at Grace Church. When a church supper or luncheon is served, there is a saucer under the coffee cup. Now that's hardly earth-shaking, even in these days when congregations may have long since parted with all chinaware in the church kitchen in favor of paper plates or the services of caterers. But think about it: Do we serve guests at home with paper plates and plastic cups? Why, then, should a different standard prevail for table fellow-ship among Christians, a tradition that dates back to biblical times? Is there a hint of phony sophistication in saucers? None intended. I testify to thoroughly enjoying *ugali* (an African version of cornmeal mush), yams, and a glass of Tang served with genuine hospitality in a congregation in a remote Kenyan village—without plates or flatware of any kind, let alone cups and saucers or running water in which to wash them. My hosts were doing their best, and their best was excellent in every way. But we're not in rural Kenya. We owe it to God and each other to do our best in our way. In the early 21st century are people too busy to get into the church kitchen and wash dishes after meals? Do modern women resent being relegated to the kitchen? It's not beyond this pastor, the Rev. Dr. himself, to tie an apron around my middle and start in on a stack of dirty dishes. Many of us learned much about our families while doing chores around the house. The church kitchen is a no less promising place for listening to and learning what doesn't always reach pastoral ears in more traditional settings. Doing things with the best we can bring is part of our life in Christ, and that applies to items small and modest as well as to those great and noble. Excellence belongs in little things, even things as small as a saucer under the cup. But what that saucer stands for is much more than a style in serving.

Excellence becomes contagious in a congregation as it is demonstrated at every level and modeled in pastoral leadership. I've seen it expressed in countless ways. A skilled insurance executive superintended our Sunday school for a decade with high standards and skills imported from his daily vocation. That meant close collaboration with me in selecting and training teachers. It meant regular rounds of class visitations to get a feel for how teachers and children were doing. It meant finding people who could advise him effectively on Sunday-school materials and the soundness of their content, an essential interest that I shared with him. It meant regular meetings to encourage and motivate teachers to be at their best, because he was doing his best for them. And it meant tactfully steering volunteers who were long on willingness but short on aptitude for teaching to other areas of parish life where they might excel.

Excellence is a beautiful thing to see spreading throughout the church. A plumber comes to mind, one who kept our boilers and pipes in good shape for years and never sent us a bill. (A trustee's comment: "Pastors are useful, yes, but give me a plumber who will come out on Saturday night and fix a busted pipe.") Think of the electricians and carpenters who volunteer skills of excellence. And members who offer excellence in church choirs, Sunday after Sunday, year after year. Excellence is a key to navigating our way in pastoral leadership through the minefields of the worship wars. Whether traditional or contemporary or a combination, excellence in music and soundness in theological content should set the standard. Where else do people gather to sing these days, and how else can they learn the richness of liturgy and hymnody to worship God, if not by participating in thoughtfully planned, carefully executed worship? Excellence in handling church offerings and in budget-setting is all the more paramount in our day, when giant corporations fall victim to incompetence and criminal shenanigans. Of course, the church comes in for its share of well-publicized misdeeds. This fact must make us all the more alert to the need for the chief and foremost treasure given us, the confession of sin and Christ's forgiveness offered to the penitent.

On and on the list goes, with room for any number of additions. Planning a church building or an evangelism outreach, recruiting potential candidates for pastoral ministry, training laity as Stephen ministers to serve those with particular needs, sustaining a first-rate adult education program, finding ways to give high schoolers a taste of mission involvement abroad or at home, supporting farmers who set aside acres whose harvest goes to mission causes, preparing couples for marriage, keeping the nursery spotless, or staying with those whose dying is a long agony—these are among the signs of excellence in a congregation not willing to settle for second best.

Practicing excellence is not elitism. It is putting God's love to work in ways that show every person counts—and in a context where tensions are faced, where successes are celebrated, where the best is sought though never fully achieved. Excellence comes from the Savior who is known, loved, and served; whose Spirit sends people from Sunday worship equipped for excellence in discipleship in their between-Sundays world. In that weekday realm where excellence can shine but where mediocrity is too common, where grasping rather than giving can become the norm, where everything has a price and nothing a value, excellence is an oasis in a wasteland. We owe our best in giving ourselves to God in response to all he has given us.

> Finally, beloved, whatever is true, whatever is honorable, whatever is just, whatever is pure, whatever is pleasing, whatever is commendable, if there is any excellence and if there is anything worthy of praise, think about these things. Keep on doing the things that you have learned and received and heard and seen in me, and the God of peace will be with you.
>   Philippians 4:8–9

The subject of virtue in pastoral life is set forth in this chapter by attention to accountability, authority, creative fidelity, ethics, integrity, patience, and excellence. These are not separate qualities, but inevitably woven together as they stem from the indwelling Spirit of God. Thus they are ours not because we deserve them as people of moral superiority but because they come to us as a gift. We receive and use them not as solo actors, but in community with God's faithful people in congregations for whose sake we are called.

3

Pastor and People

WE MIGHT BE TEMPTED TO ASSUME THAT PASTOR AND PEOPLE love and care for each other. That does not go without saying, however. It needs saying most emphatically that mutual care by pastor and people for their common life under God is the constant responsibility of both, as well as a joy and privilege. Neglect of one another spells trouble. When a coldness or a disconnect of any sort puts distance between God's people and those who serve them, ministry suffers. The long-suffering of parishioners who bear with difficult pastors comes through in the wry humor of the story about the preacher who startled the congregation after the benediction one Sunday. He scowled at the people, leaned forward from the pulpit, and declared in a gruff tone: "The Jesus who brought me to this congregation 33 years ago is the same Jesus who is leading me on to another congregation. I'm leaving!" The congregation rose as one and sang with unconcealed relief: "What a Friend We Have in Jesus!" No doubt there is a parallel story for pastors who have been worn out by contentious, sniping, hard-to-love congregations.

Pastors and people belong to each other not because it's easy but because our sins are forgiven. This blessing is where the power is found for pastors and people to bear, believe, hope, and endure all things, as the lyric words of Paul attest (1 Cor. 13:7). I bear witness to the fruits of that love, which I experienced in my four-plus decades serving one congregation. Of course, these dynamics can be experienced in pastorates of short duration. It's also true that staying in one place for a long time does not in itself ensure growth and depth. If 25 or

50 years pass without much change, pastor and people might simply repeat one year's experience 25 or 50 times over and steadily spiral down into stagnation and deterioration. Some things, however, can best be learned in depth by seeing them at work in one congregation over a sustained period of time. These I want to share because I have known the joy and sheer goodness of God's leavening grace abundantly given to pastor and people in our corner of the Lord's vineyard. These qualities of relating to people, though not limited to the church, will almost certainly evolve when a congregation and a pastor work together regardless of the number of years. Here, then, are instances from one pastoral ministry, offered to stir the imagination and enlarge the promise of ministry through relationships well grounded in grace.

Friendship

We met in 1947. I recall something of the brief conversation in the seminary quadrangle where we both were first-year students. In a few sentences, we agreed to be roommates the next year. Thus began a friendship that over the years has developed to the point where the adjective "best" is not a misfit. It may sound like name-dropping to say that the friend described is Martin E. Marty, but such is not intended. Almost six decades ago, we were just two students who decided to team up to break the pattern of graduates from feeder schools rooming together. What began as a spur-of-the-moment decision has grown into a deep and lasting friendship, enriching in ways well beyond anything we could have imagined when it began.

We are both pastors, my calling centered in the congregation and Marty's in the classroom. Our friendship as two people who happen to be ordained does not suggest that "pastoral friendship" is something categorically different from other friendships, any more than one could speak of a pastoral pair of shoes, pastoral toothpaste, or a pastoral credit card. Yet, as all of us know who are called to ministry, certain aspects of friendship take on particular meaning in our lives. As I speak of them, I am mindful that I am but one of many women and men in ministry who know what I am talking about.

First, we need friendship for the sake of our survival. "We have friends so that we don't get killed." I quote that striking line from a book of Marty's on friendship, and it suggests pointedly why deep friendships are essential in life [Martin E. Marty, *Friendship* (Allen, Texas: Argus, 1980, p. 7)]. Made as we all are in the image of God, whose very Being is triune and thus social in the ultimate meaning of the term, we are made for relationships. Friendship ranks high in those relationships that make and keep us humane. Without it, something essential in us dies. "We have friends so that we don't get killed" makes that point by allusion to lethal military combat, where a buddy's shout of warning or the act of shielding a friend with one's own body means survival rather than death. In human life in general, we only have to think of a friendless life to understand what is killed off inside the human spirit without relationships.

I believe that what makes the Lueking-Marty friendship enduring is that neither of us seeks to cross boundaries by laying claim to the other jealously, competitively, or possessively. C. S. Lewis wrote a classic essay titled "The Inner Ring," in which he traced the way friendship begins and thrives because of natural, shared interests, as well as the way friendship dies because of the subtle sin of exploiting the other through self-serving motives. I've learned much from Marty and a host of other friends whose have generously shared their gifts of mind and spirit with me. Early on in my pastoral ministry, I hit a major snag of doubt about my worthiness to continue in the pastoral calling. I called my friend at midnight, and he made time to hear me out and console me with the gospel in the early hours of the day. In later years, when Elsa Marty was terminally ill, it was my turn to be there for him.

Our families have shared many happy hours at picnics, camping outings, and holiday dinners. We've respected the boundaries necessary to good friendship. We've made the efforts needed to tend our friendship by not taking each other for granted. It's been a natural, unforced, mutually enjoyable, freely formed bond that is no small sign of divine grace. The bottom line is that we're better people for helping each other mature, each of us in our calling as a person, husband, father, pastor, theologian—and friend.

Jaroslav Pelikan has asked why theologians have not addressed friendship as a subject that belongs in the wide realm of Christian truth. Our Lord himself has called us not servants but friends (John 15:15). And yet in the vast numbers of theological books and manuals on canon law that have followed down through the centuries, references to Jesus's followers as "servants" outnumber any reference to them as "friends" by more than 50-fold. Pelikan has noted the oddity that we must turn to Cicero's *De amicitia* rather than to theological works for an extended reflection on friendship.

What may be missing from theological books must not be missing from pastoral practice if the pastor is to remain whole in body and spirit. I have been immensely blessed by good friends within and beyond Grace Church and could not envision my calling without the leaven of friends. Perhaps the finest commentary on friendship between pastor and people is that in the past several years of retirement, I have not felt it necessary to sever friendship ties with many whom I have served as pastor. I treasure the fact that my pastoral successor at Grace, Bruce Modahl, is my friend, a man with whom I share a mutually respectful and nourishing relationship. I keep out of his way in matters that have to do with his place as pastor of the congregation and am clear about the fact that I am no longer the pastor at Grace. The added fact that I chose to live on another continent during most of the first six years after Bruce arrived is a mark of friendship as well as a guard against my giving the impression of meddling. We are friends because we both belong to the Lord who calls us his friends. For that reason we are no threat to each other, but on the contrary support, appreciate, and love each other.

Admonition belongs in friendship. People who achieve heights of fame and power are imperiled if their ascent has cost them friendships along the way. "A friend is one who warns you," a Jewish proverb says—and how many people have crashed disastrously because they never allowed a friend to warn them! If it's lonely at the top, it is because those anxiously perched up there have made it so by shedding friendships, treating people like disposable gum wrappers. We fail our friends if we deny them the truth they're missing. The pastoral calling puts us in a very public position, like it or not, and blessed are those who love us enough to warn us when we start careering toward some precipice. It need not be a dramatic cliff, either. Friends have told me simply: "Dean, be still and let others talk." Or, "Dean, don't try to win arguments in public." Or, "Dean, do you know how much you're biting off and how much you can chew?" Or even, "Dean, your fly is open."

Friends can lighten the load when pastoral work seems extra heavy. That happens as they rescue us from introspection with humor that lifts the gloom. Gustav Weigel, a premier Catholic theologian a few decades back, was in a blue-funk mood and altogether uncooperative with the hospital staff after suffering a serious heart attack. His good friend, also a Catholic theologian, came to his hospital bed as friend and spiritual brother. Weigel refused to open his eyes and made no response to John Courtney Murray's solicitous inquiry. After some moments of getting nowhere with Weigel, Murray leaned close to his friend's ear and said: "Gus, if you die on me now, I'll never speak to you again!" When Weigel's lips began to quiver with laughter he could not suppress, he was on his way to recovery and years of useful vocation.

Friendship, in this case blessed by humor, found a way to embody the grace that heals. *We have friends, and we are friends, so that we don't get killed.*

Collegiality

Jesus never sent his disciples out alone but always two by two. Paul was never a lone ranger on his missionary journeys but always traveled in partnership with Barnabas or Silas or others named in the Book of Acts.

Thus, from its biblical origins on through the centuries of the church's history, pastoral ministry is collegial to its very core. It offers more than the obvious morale boosting, shared workload, the capacity to reach more people, and the like. The real point of collegiality is that in our partnership, we practice what we preach. By the quality of our relationships as colleagues in the Word, people can see the truth of the gospel expressed not only in our talking about forgiveness but in our forgiving each other, not just in our calls for patience but in our forbearing each other. This demonstration in deeds is what makes our words sound and trustworthy. Parishioners are keen to pick up on that.

We have no choice but to be accountable for the quality of our teamwork as a credible recommendation of the truth we proclaim. The term "pastoral prima donna" ought to be regarded as an oxymoron. Petty quarrels, backbiting, jealousies, and willful neglect of each other come under withering denunciation in the New Testament. Paul wrote: "Put away from you all bitterness and wrath and anger and wrangling and slander, together with all malice, and be kind to one another, tenderhearted, forgiving one another, as God in Christ has forgiven you" (Eph. 4:31–32). Too much is at stake to take each other for granted or deliberately to undermine each other's gifts in our calling to serve in bringing the body of believers to full maturity in Christ.

Collegiality was already well at work in the Grace staff when I became a part of it. Working with music ministers and the teaching staff in our parish school was a privilege second to none through the years. The same can be said of shared ministry with the dozen assistant and associate pastors who served with me from 1954 until 1998. I experienced collegiality through the patience and loyalty of the church secretaries and janitors and other ministry partners without whose skills and commitment my daily work would have been unmanageable.

Collegiality grew through weekly staff worship, the key to keeping a sense that each of us did not simply have a job but all of us shared a partnership in service as each was gifted. While I know that other concepts of parish administration can work very well, I belong to the school that says there is one pastor rather than co-pastors, and that it is the pastor's responsibility to instill collegiality throughout the staff. That idea may sound contradictory, but in practice I found it otherwise. As I demonstrated support, care, admonition, and vision in collegial relationships with each staff member, so they practiced such relationships with one another. It was an affirmation of my role to see that as the pastor I was not the only one enabling others to live the spirit of the gospel in relating to each other. Collegiality is a gift of the Spirit, wonderfully multiplied as it is received and practiced by all who share by speech and action in the ministry of the gospel.

I didn't choose the hymns and choral anthems for Sunday worship, but I cherished the regular meetings with musician Paul Bouman, whose talents in matching hymns with sermon texts were superior to mine, as well as exploring with him what was best and not best in newer forms of worship. The ministry of music can be a nightmare when pastors and church musicians do not respect one another, and too many congregations are littered with the debris of battles between the two. I did not have to run Grace Lutheran School. My pastoral role was to meet regularly with the principal, Gerald Koenig, and before him, Victor Waldschmidt, to see how our respective ministries served the larger good of the parish. As our staff grew, adding women as well as men in key roles, collegiality became all the more necessary and challenging. Having had such genuinely satisfying collegial relationships with the music and school ministries in my first 20 years, I was naive in assuming that it would be the same later on. What happened was in fact a wider, deeper experience of the Spirit's work of building collegiality when later staff relationships were far more complicated and challenging. Even so, the essentials of mutual forgiveness and support carried us through new circumstances involving more people with other gifts and the inevitable tensions that go with them.

Collegiality at the congregational level, in my view, meets its sternest test when facing the need to dismiss clergy or other staff people. Terminating a person from a staff position with collegiality intact means doing what must be done in fairness and in partnership with those assigned such oversight in the congregation. I found this task to be the hardest part of ministry but learned the hard way that nothing is gained by living in denial of endless incompetence or deliberate disruptiveness. After all, the apostles Paul and Barnabas came head-to-head over taking John Mark as a partner on the second missionary journey and parted ways over the sharp disagreement (Acts 15:36–41). They did the necessary thing, forming separate teams for separate mission journeys. Why do we hesitate and procrastinate so often in facing up to the human frailties that appear in our collegial work today? I believe this behavior comes from the illusion that there are no mismatched partners in serving the people of God.

Collegiality is not limited to professional staff partners. It spreads across the whole spectrum of pastoral connections to all who serve as elected officers of the congregation as well as to teachers of children, workers with youth, helpers with building maintenance, visitors to the sick and shut-in, and all others who make congregations unique on earth. It is my understanding that more than half the Christian congregations in our country have no paid staff beyond the pastor; these are the settings where collegiality as partnership of pastors with laity is best known.

Collegiality also often reaches beyond the walls of the congregation. I enjoyed a most meaningful experience of collegiality with a group of a dozen or so Protestant and Roman Catholic clergy who met each Friday morning from seven till nine for breakfast, prayer, and study of the lectionary lessons for the Sunday 10 days hence. Each week one of us would host the breakfast and lead the textual studies, with all contributing insights into the biblical passages at hand. Thus, we helped each other prime the pump for preaching one of the Scripture lessons. While theological differences were not avoided, neither did we dwell on them. Most often, we shared edifying insights and learning that arose from our daily practice of ministry in our congregations and our communities. In addition, while we kept our Friday-morning sessions focused on preaching, it occasionally happened that one or another of us would find a moment when it was right to speak of some personal or pastoral burden that the strong bond of trust among us could bear. I looked forward to these Friday mornings for 25 years and found them to be the most meaningful experience of ecumenical collegiality I have ever known. I am glad that the group still continues and wish it could be the model for all ecumenical relationships. It has ever puzzled me that as often as I have advocated the value of this group to other clergy, I am not aware that such clergy study groups are common elsewhere.

If I could start again as a newly ordained pastor, I would foster a keener sense of knowing the place of collegiality when facing unwelcome realities, such as problematic people either unprepared or not gifted for their work in the congregation. And certainly I would ask God to make me more aware of the daily blessing of joy in shared work, shared gifts, and shared friendships with those I've been privileged to call colleagues. As I look back over my years, I can see now what too often I took for granted, the sheer goodness of working together with so many men and women whose faith, hope, and love still bless me.

Availability

Among the most influential teachers I have had in my life was one who posted a sign above his office door: ENTER WITHOUT KNOCKING. I did. Often. Always with benefit. It was an early experience in learning the grace of availability.

Over the years, whenever appropriate, I worked with my study door open. It is a symbol of something always apparent in Jesus's ministry, his availability to all kinds of people, everywhere, all the time. Of course, more often than not, this habit nettled his disciples, who sought to limit his availability. But Jesus made himself available on the terms that were his: as the One bringing in the kingdom of his Father, not waiting for the world to come on its terms to the saving reign of God.

Availability begins not with an open door but with an open mind. It is an attitude, a quality of heart, a willingness to meet people on their terms and timetable. It means preparing for surprises, leaving time each day for the unexpected along with the duties that must be sensibly planned and carried out. At heart, availability is love for people, born of the gospel itself.

Availability is easily misused. It can stem from the flawed sense of needing to be needed. Early on in my ministry I learned that I could fool myself into avoiding responsibilities that require sustained, uninterrupted time (sermon writing comes to mind) by taking calls and making visits that could just as well wait. People can abuse pastoral availability when they are eager to hear themselves talk but have no intention of listening to what they need to hear. And being available takes a toll on time with spouse and family, a problem that I experienced when attempting to establish regular days off and other times set apart for those dear to me. I found that being available to walk-ins by street people required more than my time; when appropriate, the situation called for referring people to the skills and services of agencies better suited than mine to dealing with survival problems. I had to learn the skill that the late, great Cardinal Joseph Bernardin expressed when telling his driver before arriving at one of the myriad events he had to take in every day: "Now remember, the important thing is to get us out of here as soon as possible." Time is not endless, nor is availability. That said, I do look back with gratitude for interruptibility more often than not. The word *pastor*, after all, means shepherd. Sheep are not known for being organized and on time. And, as every pastor knows, going the second mile to practice availability does not always lead to outcomes we anticipate.

Two stories of availability come to mind.

Vesely knocked on my study door one summer day. He began—as most walk-ins did—describing a situation of desperation. He was a refugee from Serbian Yugoslavia, living in Chicago, working, and handling his own room and board, all of which set him apart from most who came to our door in dire straits. His face was a road map of anguish as he told his story of bad news just received from his wife in Eastern Europe. His younger son, a boy of 10, had been run over and killed by a car when coming home from school. Vesely was desperate to get home for the funeral and to be with his wife and family. He showed me the airline ticket for a flight leaving Chicago for Vienna within hours, and gave me the airline phone number to confirm his ticket, plus the phone number of his landlord, plus that of his employer. What he lacked was $200 to get a train ticket from Vienna to his home in Yugoslavia. Would I lend him the money? He had found his way to our door through a policeman who had pointed out our church tower rising high above the trees. I checked out all the numbers, and those who spoke with me confirmed his story. So I found the needed money in a pastoral discretionary fund, gave it to him, instructed him to return to me when he got back to Chicago, and sent him on his way—wondering if I would ever see him again.

He did return two weeks later, with photographs of his son's casket banked in flowers in the back of a pickup truck, on its way to the cemetery. He expressed his thanks, talked a bit about his life, and asked about the schedule of payments by which he could repay the loan—all of which was exceptional. My batting average is next to nil on loan recipients coming back, and no one had ever signed on for loan repayments.

As it happened, we needed custodial help at the time. I asked if he was interested and what his skills were. After our business manager and trustee board interviewed him, he got the job. He worked consistently and well, paying back the loan in full in less than the allotted time. Moreover, he joined the adult instruction class and made his spiritual home with us at Grace.

For over a year, all went well. It was one of those experiences that kept me available rather than cynical about the next person in need.

I was away from Grace for three months on sabbatical. The first news to greet me when I returned was that Vesely had disappeared. No one knew his whereabouts. But soon phone calls began to come in from those wanting to know where the man was who had borrowed $35, or $110, or $350. It became evident that Vesely was placing bets at the track in amounts increasingly beyond what he could handle. His solution was to vanish. He was as good at disappearing as he was artful in hiding his deeply embedded gambling addiction. I have no idea where he is today.

I cannot regret being available to him when he came to the church door. How much of his story about his son's death was true or false I leave to God. He did pay back the money lent him. He did work hard with us. He did renew his baptismal covenant and join the congregation. The jolt of his disappearance and unpaid loans to others should not have come as a total shock. Paul speaks of the civil war between the redeemed nature and the sinful nature constantly going on in all Christians. Here was one more sign of it, well disguised under layers of good intentions and disastrous denial of an uncontrollable habit. God has the last word on Vesely, me, and all the rest of us. We're all traveling along and must not be thrown off course because others are derailed for reasons not always clear to us. We continue in availability not because of 20/20 vision of human need but through faithfulness to what is required of us as stewards of the mysteries of God (1 Cor. 4:2).

The other story about availability took place under vastly different circumstances. My wife, Beverly, and I were guests at an award dinner in Chicago at which the national television newsman Jim Lehrer was an honoree. It was my good fortune to be seated next to Lehrer. Always interested in people, keen journalist and interviewer that he is, he turned to me and asked what my line of work was. This was an elegant black-tie dinner;

I was dressed accordingly. No wonder he looked surprised when I told him, "I am a Lutheran pastor."

To my surprise, Lehrer fixed a steady eye on me and asked with unmistakable seriousness: "I want to know what you believe and teach about death." I gave him a five-word answer: "Death is a conquered enemy."

He paused thoughtfully and leaned forward to hear more. Since he had initiated the subject and gave every sign of wanting to know what I believed in the core of my being about death and its conqueror, I told him the good news of Jesus Christ, crucified and risen—death's conqueror, and the One who bestows power to deal with death. Death is the kind of enemy that wields retroactive power, not only holding human beings in the thrall of fear and denial long before physical death occurs but turning death into a taboo. Along those lines the conversation went.

Lehrer explained that he had lost his own father at a young age. He was never permitted to talk about what that huge loss did to him. Others told him that his dad was with Jesus and that he ought to be glad more than sad. That didn't wash with a teenager who had a gaping wound in his heart that needed healing, not denying. He went on to say that not long before, he himself had suffered a serious heart attack and came close to dying. But when he came home from the hospital, neither he nor his wife and daughters could talk about death openly and get at the real needs the subject inevitably uncovers. Here was one of the most admired, capable, and sophisticated men in American journalism, who deals in depth with every kind of problem that dominates the world's news and does so with an excellence that makes many people plan their weekday supper hour around "The NewsHour with Jim Lehrer" on PBS—and he was discussing a long-closed subject with a Lutheran preacher in a tux.

We talked further. Everything else about the evening, for both of us as it turned out, was secondary to this business of death and its conqueror. Once in a while, availability is rewarded in unexpected ways. While in Bratislava, Slovakia, several years after the Lehrer dinner meeting, I received a flurry of e-mails from friends at home who mentioned seeing Lehrer in a recently televised interview in which he made mention of the award banquet in Chicago. I was told I should see the tape when I returned, which I did. I was surprised and moved to hear Jim Lehrer speak of what he termed a life-changing experience, talking with a Lutheran pastor named Dean Something-or-other, who helped him get at the subject of death. I did not expect that. It was good to hear it, remembering that I am not the life-changer but a messenger of the One who is. I am grateful that our friendship continues through occasional exchanges of brief notes.

Availability counts, wherever and whenever the moment arrives, whether when one is meeting with parishioners, or encountering people from off the street, or having unscheduled encounters in unexpected places. Availability arises despite the unexpected, and Jesus's Parable of the Good Samaritan (Luke 10:29–37) calls us to do better than pass by on the other side.

Discernment

Discernment has to do with seeing with "the eyes of your heart enlightened," to use Paul's striking phrase from Ephesians 1:18. I hear discernment mentioned more frequently now than earlier in my ministry. It often refers to a process important in helping candidates for ordination sort out their gifts for ministry, or lack of them.

"Seeing with the eyes of your heart enlightened" has broader meaning, however. Discernment is needed all through the wide span of parish life and is especially pertinent when pastor and people work together in decisions on worship, evangelism, stewardship, counseling, and other aspects of ministry. We practice discernment when charting next steps for a course of congregational action by asking, is this action sound, timely, doable, and consistent with our faith? The answers come best when pastor and people together seek God's will when choosing this priority over that one, doing this now or waiting for that till later.

I learned how much discernment means when leading Grace Church in ministry to the homeless in our suburban area. Both parishioners and I needed to attend to God's leading as we moved forward in a mission that was soon perceived by many in our neighborhood as a threat to property values. It all began without much fanfare. A representative of a suburban-area clergy group seeking churches that would provide shelter for homeless adults and children came to me with an appeal: would Grace Church be the Saturday-night host for those needing supper and a safe place to sleep from October through April? I met with our social ministry committee. They agreed and passed the recommendation on to the church council, where approval was also given. All the while we assumed that the good people of Grace and surely most of the good people of our community would accept a decision to house the homeless as consistent with our mission.

We soon were jolted by the sobering discovery that sheltering homeless people in our school gym each Saturday night for half a year (other neighboring congregations and synagogues covered the other nights) was loudly protested and vehemently opposed by some people both outside and within Grace Church. People were threatened by the thought that "outsiders" (read "people from Chicago"), mostly minority, would be welcomed in nearby Grace Church. We who supported this work underestimated the fear that robs people from seeing homeless fellow humans with the enlightened eyes of the heart. Instead, they saw them through eyes blinded by the bottom line of property-value dollars. We failed to discern the deeper strands of sin that suddenly surface when 30 people—some of them children, many of them suburbanites suddenly caught in financial ruin—are welcomed, given a meal, bedded down, and sent on their way by seven o'clock on Sunday morning. Our failure to practice good discernment showed in our inadequate preparation of our neighbors and ourselves for what we were doing, plans for how we would proceed, and our motives for this ministry with those to whom Christ called us.

A year of sessions, first with the village board of trustees and then with our own members, was required to secure permission finally to proceed. Another mistake in discernment on my part resulted in my doing too much advocating before the town board myself, instead of enlisting more parishioners who paid plenty of taxes and had earned the right to be heard. The village board's obstruction stopped when it finally became apparent that according to the First Amendment, it could not prevent the free exercise of our religious conviction, On the Sunday when our own parishioners came together by the hundreds to vote on the resolution to house the homeless, picketers from the congregation and community were on the church steps handing out anti-homeless pamphlets to all who entered. My sermon text was from the first lesson appointed for that day, the magnificent vision of Isaiah for "sharing your bed with the hungry, and bringing the homeless poor into your house" (58:7). The discernment needed to act with consensus as a congregation was granted by the Holy Spirit. The mission was approved overwhelmingly. I was surprised to see television crews from the major Chicago networks interviewing our members as they left the meeting. What pleased me most was parishioner Adrienne Rott's summary of the day, included in one station's report: "Today love and fear clashed, and love won out." As we served homeless men and women and children over the next year, another surprise came. People of River Forest, not members of Grace, sent messages of respect and approval, some with checks included to help with costs. We learned that there are more of those who "see with the eyes of the heart" than we realized. Our Saturday-night homeless ministry continued until we began supporting a program offered by a social-work agency for training homeless people to make it on their own in independent housing—a ministry we considered more effective.

Another lesson in discernment for me and many in the congregation came when the winds of the charismatic movement that blew several decades ago were also felt at Grace Church. While other congregations struggled with divisiveness caused by misuse of charismatic gifts, a blight on Christians from the Corinthians of the New Testament era onward, we were spared such divisions. Some members with Spirit-given charisms came to me personally and spoke in tongues as we sat together in quiet prayer. Since I did not have the gift of glossolalia or of interpreting tongues, I could only acknowledge the Spirit's work in them, thank them for their trust, remind them and myself that Paul writes that the Spirit's foremost gifts are faith, hope, and love (1 Cor. 13), and thank them for not causing division by exalting themselves over others. We learned discernment together as we honored the diversity of God's gifts and were mutually encouraged by discovering how varied gifts worked for the common good of all.

We learned more about the importance of timing as a factor in discernment when the time came to call our first woman into the pastoral ministry at Grace. For more than 90 years, only men served that office at Grace. In the early 1990s, that changed. I knew Phylllis Kersten from her previous years of stellar service on the staff of the Lutheran Church–Missouri Synod Board of Missions and later with the Wheatridge Ministries, which is focused on health and healing. I admired her strength of faith, gentleness of spirit, breadth of vision, and promise for pastoral ministry following her graduation from the Lutheran School of Theology at Chicago. I spoke with her about Grace and asked her to join us in prayer to discern the right time for us to present her as a candidate for associate pastor in the congregation. The elders were enthusiastic about the prospect after meeting her, as was the church council. Lessons learned from inadequate preparation for our homeless ministry several years before prompted me to prepare materials for the entire congregation to study and discuss in open meetings called for that purpose. After varied concerns were heard and all had opportunity to speak, a near-unanimous consensus was reached. Phyllis Kersten was installed as our associate pastor on July 14, 1996.

My successor at Grace has been much more intentional about helping Grace members discern whether they are called to professional church work. Soon after he arrived, Bruce Modahl established a committee for this purpose. He found able leadership for it, naming Cindy Halvorson as chair. I have enjoyed being included in the committee to help plan events for those with signs of aptitude for the pastoral and teaching ministry. In such initiatives for lifting up ministerial prospects, the congregation is viewed as a prime resource in finding and encouraging those with promise. It often happens that young people, indeed people of all ages, do not realize their potential for a lifetime of service in the kingdom until someone tells them about it.

All of us in pastoral ministry have our own stories of how someone or something helped us discern God's call. In my case it came in a rural congregation I attended late in the summer after my high-school graduation. After a full Sunday of bailing hay on my uncle's farm where I was working, he announced that the family, including me, should get cleaned up for an evening mission festival service in a country church near Rockford, Illinois. I was less than thrilled and went with no sense that a life-changing moment was at hand. A young chaplain from a nearby army camp preached that evening. The hymn following the sermon was from the 19th century Protestant missionary tradition, "Hark, the Voice of Jesus Calling." The first and last verses ended with "Here am I, send me, Send me." No lightning from heaven struck, nor was I overcome by a surge of emotion. I simply sang the phrase, then thought it was meant for me. The next day I sent my parents a postcard, stating my hunch that I'd like to become a pastor. Before the end of that last week of August 1945, I had returned home, talked with my parents and pastor, and found myself enrolled in a small Lutheran college in southwest Kansas that I did not know existed until the day before I arrived, a week late, on the campus. I marvel now at how unexpectedly the circumstances of that call to ministry came to me and how the phrase at the end of a hymn verse nudged me toward discerning God's call in it. From that moment on, I have not had five minutes' regret for what was given so graciously, quietly, and effectively. The memory of that experience has kept me open to the mysterious ways in which the Spirit of God calls people to ministry. Sometimes discernment of that call comes after years of waiting in prayer for the eyes of the heart to be enlightened. Sometimes the call comes through intentional parish cultivation by those who encourage prospects to recognize capacities in themselves they do not yet see. Sometimes discerning the call of God can come in hearing a sermon or singing a hymn that carries life-changing power. But in every case, discernment is a work of divine grace in which the eyes of the heart are opened to see "the hope to which he has called us . . . and . . . the immeasurable greatness of his power for those who believe" (Eph. 1:18–19).

Hospitality

Let all guests be received as Christ, a motto from the Benedictine tradition, has been on our front door for years. These seven words sum up an essential of Christian living, as well as a staple of the pastoral life and household.

Perhaps it is because we have had much experience in being welcomed near and far that hospitality figures largely in our ministry. I say "our" because my wife has been so essential in providing the major effort that it requires. Time after time over the years, family, friends, strangers, parishioners, foster children, foreign students, travelers, and people who had nowhere to stay have received Beverly's welcome. She makes it look easy, the hallmark of doing it with love. That's especially true when hospitality has needed more than social manners to sustain it.

On one occasion early in our marriage, I was needed at a court session to determine placement for three children of a troubled family. The judge sent them home with me temporarily. They sometimes jumped off our attached garage roof to avoid visits from their mother, who would come just before supper with sweets to spoil their appetite. Another child appeared at our door one night, tired of being kept up late to mix drinks when her mother was too drunk to do it herself. In such cases, hospitality from Beverly and all of us with her was stretched from several days to several months before a more permanent placement could be arranged. Not easy. One of our foster children (there have been 32 over the years) stayed with us for three years. It was a challenge for our own children to understand why adjustment to family living was hard for him (he came from a tragically disordered family). Works of hospitality require far more than feel-good motives, however. It takes nothing less than the power of God the Holy Spirit, sent by the Father through his Son's redeeming hospitality, to welcome us all into the household of God. That motive applies no less when preparing for unexpected Sunday visitors, or 25 guests on special occasions, or a foster baby's two o'clock in the morning feeding, or late arrivals who will occupy our guest room. Hospitality needs the sturdy stuff of stamina, intelligence, planning, flexibility, organization, delegation, and above all, love as the motive. Amid the increasing facelessness of modern, anonymous living, Romans 15:7 is all the more needed: *Welcome one another, therefore, just as Christ has welcomed you, for the glory of God.*

We know the blessing of hospitality as receivers, too. On a sabbatical visit to Nepal, we rented a motorcycle in Katmandu to follow around our missionary physician host, Richard Matern. In the confusion of people, cars, cows, and carts in the crowded streets, we lost him on his motor scooter ahead of us just as the sun was setting. To be a little more accurate, I overturned the Suzuki while avoiding a schoolchild who had darted into my path, with no serious injury except to our dignity as we sprawled on the pavement—with our host far out of our sight and unaware of our predicament. We had no choice but to stay put in the hope that Dr. Matern would find us. Near our street-corner location was a fruit stand with a single lightbulb over it, the only light available. The man in charge noticed our plight and rightly guessed that we were foreigners in a jam. Before closing up for the night, he politely asked us, in good English, if he might help. Hearing our explanation, he offered to take us into his home for the night. That spontaneous gesture impressed me as no small sign of providential hospitality from a Buddhist Nepalese to a Lutheran pastor and wife facing a long night sitting on the curb of a very dark street in an Asian city totally strange to us. It also made me wonder how he would have fared in reverse circumstances if he had been stuck on a Chicago street at a late-night hour, and how many offers—in Nepali—he would have received as a total stranger halfway around the world from home? After several hours of waiting, we did finally make our way back to Matern's house via a route I do not remember. What I shall always remember is the offer by that proprietor of a fruit stand whose hospitality radiated a light brighter than the 40-watt bulb over his stand. Such experiences have taught us the grace of receiving as well as giving hospitality.

Congregational hospitality is essential to evangelism as well as to the complexities of interfaith encounters. It is no less vital to ongoing spiritual growth as people rightly measure the parish by the genuineness with which each person's gifts are welcomed and deployed. The larger the congregation, the greater the task. Many megachurches do exceptionally well in showing hospitality to those who are new to the gospel and life in Christ. At Grace we have much to learn, while we also have come a good distance. Greeters welcome strangers at the door, and these guests leave after worship with a loaf of welcome bread symbolizing the Bread of Life we seek to share. Grace leaders have made much more effort in recent years to integrate people into the nurture and mission of the congregation. Ways of doing this necessarily vary, of course. In every case, however, hospitality is the gift, art, aptitude, and awareness that enable us to reach out and welcome without overdoing it with those who are clearly put off by too effusive a welcome. I recall the comment of a gay man who, after years of testing us as an acutely observant visitor, told me that it was the hospitable spirit of an 80-year-old widow next to him in the pew that opened the door for him at Grace.

The plethora of strategies for implementing small groups in congregations signals the growing awareness of how much hospitality means in the Christian story. Each effort is effective to the extent that it embodies the spirit of Mary and Martha and Lazarus in that Bethany household where our Lord found a welcome respite from the near-constant accusatory atmosphere of Jerusalem. Hospitality deserves greater appreciation in theological work on Christianity and world religions. Muslim hospitality, clearly called for in the Koran, is a sign of God at work when it is sincerely expressed. So is the timeless call of Israel's prophets to welcome the stranger by remembering the former days as aliens in Egypt. That Buddhist shopkeeper in Katmandu and his many Buddhist compatriots I have come to know in Japan under other circumstances testify to God's welcoming in a world dangerously adrift. Indeed, people with no religion are called into the hospitable purposes of the living God who knows them though they may not know him, as the Bible teaches throughout.

Years ago I gained insights into hospitality from the Italian exegete and churchman Romano Guardini. Among the most memorable is his comment on what it will mean when each of us rounds the final bend of life and moves out into the loneliness and vast mystery of death and what follows. Then, he reminds us, we will know with a vengeance what hospitality means as the welcoming grace at the gate of eternal life. Who will not be astonished by the endless surprises of earthly hospitality finally revealed in its fullness as a sign of Christ's gracious presence all the way along? Then, to recall our Benedictine doorplate, the message will be not that all guests are received *as* Christ, but *by* the welcoming Christ himself, face to face.

Humor

Humor, which is after all part of our creation, belongs in pastoral ministry. Where did the idea originate that God is haunted by the possibility that somebody, somewhere, is having a good time?

There is laughter in the Bible, if we can sort it out from the pie-in-the-face versions. The Biblical picture of Jonah, savoring the prospect of the wicked people of Ninevah going up in smoke, gets comfortable in his homemade box seat just east of the city and waits to see the show. His pouting about the sunburn *he* suddenly suffers is just the extension of his real agitation with God, who is going to save the heathen of the city after all (Jonah 4:6–11). That picture can't help but bring a smile, which prepares us well for the main point that follows: divine mercy is so much greater than Jonah's narrow, carping understanding of it. Jesus's parable of the guests invited to the wedding feast (Matt. 22:1ff) features excuses that are humorous precisely because they contain the soul of humor—the improbable. Can a newly married man *not* go to the banquet because his wife won't let him out of the house? The very thought of it brings a smile, after which Jesus moves to a serious point.

Humor is a useful gift in pastoral ministry. Wilfred Kruse was a Grace member of deep faith, keen mind, and droll wit, whose sense of opportune timing in injecting humor into tense meetings was a boon when we needed it. When several hundred parishioners would gather for deliberation on the growing conflict between Grace and the denomination, feelings would inevitably run high. Without ever trying to be funny, Kruse could relieve almost palpable tensions by stating relevant wisdom with just the right touch of drollness. He was never sarcastic, never mean-spirited, never silly, but always to the point. Such a light touch helped us think straight and act faithfully without taking ourselves so seriously that we could no longer smile *at ourselves*. That's what humor as a part of faith makes possible and what qualifies it as a gift to be valued in pastoral life and work.

I borrowed from Wilfred Kruse's gift of humor as relief for tight moments. It was useful when I could offer couples preparing for marriage, nervous and unsure when sitting down with me in my study, something gently humorous that set them at ease—such as how I met my wife on a blind date as a lead-in to how *they* met. From time to time, I would begin a church council meeting by passing around a good cartoon that helped us start well. (*New Yorker* magazine references to clergy at the church door were always winners.) Humor was always welcome when teaching children and confirmands, especially when I was the butt of the joke. The favorite, which always worked, was a true story of my departure from Japan after two years of internship there prior to ordination. A group of Bible-class students came to the airport to see me off. In typical Japanese fashion, they gave me a bouquet of flowers. Their attached note was heartfelt, though written in slightly awkward English. They did well expressing their thanks and kind wishes until they came to my name, which they had previously seen only in Japanese letters. Instead of Dean Lueking, they wrote "Dum Looking."

Humor in preaching is a tricky subject because it is so subjective. There is only one Garrison Keillor, and attempts to mimic him in the pulpit are a sure disaster. Quoting this genius is another thing, and many do it beneficially. The main thing, it seems to me, is that humor, whether Keillor's or somebody else's or one's own, needs to support, not distract from, the point at hand; needs to be human, not sarcastic; is often best offered when the preacher is the butt of the joke; and must not be overdone. It can never be a substitute for substance in preaching. People do not come to church for jokes. If humor helps listening, enhances a grasp of the human condition, enlarges the setting for the word of grace to work in the church and world, then fine. I find that such humor often comes unplanned. If I get my syntax twisted or forget the offering altogether (not once but twice over the years), let the egg on my face show and let all relax momentarily with humor. The goal is to move on with everyone on board, not sidetracked.

Interestingly, what constitutes humor in preaching is culturally determined to a large extent. An American megachurch congregation of people mostly under 35 is much more attuned to humor in worship than a congregation in Japan or Slovakia, where formality is far more the style. I've heard humor wonderfully woven into preaching in Kenya, and witnessed preaching in Nanjing where apparently no one expects or needs it. For pastoral ministry anywhere, it pays to know the territory and to respect the cultural expectations.

Grace-filled humor has its place even when death is at hand. I think of Augusta Cimaglio, several months past her 100th birthday, rounding at last the final bend of life. I joined her three daughters around her hospital bed when she and we knew the end was nearing. Leaning down close to her ear, I asked, "Gussie, can you hear me?" She opened one eye and nodded yes. Then she looked up at the faces surrounding her, opened the other eye, scrutinizing each daughter's face with just the hint of a smile. I asked her if she wanted to say anything to them. Her closing words: "Too much lipstick." Augusta: the quintessential mother to the very last moment after decades of superb mothering! Her humor was her witness that the sting has been taken out of death, and by the grace of Christ we can close our eyes in peace, even with the hint of a smile.

Dignity

A seconds-long glance at the face of Pavel Uhorskai, a notable alumnus of the Lutheran seminary in Bratislava, Slovakia, where I taught during four years of my post-retirement ministry, make me think deeply about dignity.

I had stopped in one day at the offices of the Evangelical Church of the Augsburg Confession, as Lutherans identify themselves in Slovakia (a title Martin Luther would much prefer over "Lutheran"). As I entered the building, I saw a man who immediately, effortlessly communicated an unmistakable air of dignity, which came through not primarily in his somewhat regal carriage—a tall frame, ramrod straight for his years—or in his well-worn black suit that fit him well, or the black homburg he wore. It was his face that bespoke dignity. Its deep lines, aquiline nose, slightly arched eyebrows, firm chin and mouth set somewhere between solemnity and kindness, were not posed. Dignity came up from some deep wellspring and flowed outward, especially through his face.

I had only the briefest glance at him before walking on. But a few minutes later, I stopped in my tracks, remembering that I had seen that face years earlier, on the back cover of the book he wrote and translated into English under the title

Uncompromising Faith. I'm sorry that I missed speaking to him, since he died not long afterward.

The late Pavel Uhorskai was a Slovak Lutheran pastor who endured imprisonment and torture during 1949–1953, when an excessively hard-line Communist Party in what was then Czechoslovakia (separated into Slovakia and the Czech Republic since 1993) did its utmost to oppress to prove its loyalty to the Kremlin. His imprisonment was followed by years of forced labor, which he endured without capitulating to the communist manipulations of both church and state. He was granted amnesty in 1959, but it was 30 years, three prime decades of his life, before he was reinstated to the public ministry when communism fell in 1989. In 1990 his stature as a churchman was recognized by the 450,000 Slovak Lutherans (8 percent of the 5.5 million population of Slovakia), who named him general bishop.

He was a model of dignity that came as the fruit of discipleship, born of bearing the cross given him through a power beyond himself. It was forged in doing the faithful rather than the expedient thing. His face was a road map of a life lived by the costly grace of Christ crucified and risen with the wounds still in his hands.

That face offers a lesson in dignity for us all. In some fashion or another, a vibrant, tested faith shows through on our faces, indeed our whole being. Augustine exhorted every Christian to be, as he put it, "a hallelujah from head to foot." One place to look for it is certainly in the faces of those who are veterans of the cross, people whose quiet dignity runs deep and is lasting.

I offer a suggestion here that does not require overseas travel or contact with those who have suffered physically under tyrannies. It concerns an item useful but hardly essential to parish life, the pictorial directory. The faces spread across those pages help us remember people's names, of course—but much more. It is well to reflect upon those faces as a road map to the dignity bestowed upon each Christian by baptismal grace, when the forehead was marked by the sign of the cross and sealed by the Holy Spirit—forever. That dignity is being matured in those pictured, whose discipleship in times glad and sad, in times known and unknown, comes back to us as we think of them. Seeing those faces again, in a pictorial album or in person in the daily rounds, can prompt us to name these people before God in intercessory prayer. Such use of a membership directory can also serve as a reminder that parishioners pray for us pastors, a charism too often forgotten when we see ourselves only as caregivers and miss the reality of our need to receive care. Such a message, mediated by something as ordinary as a pictorial directory, bolsters us in moments of low morale or when burnout threatens. It also corrects us when the dignity of the pastoral calling is diminished by temptations to substitute glad-handing gimmickry for the straightforward handing on of the Word of life, in season and out of season. The souls represented by the faces on those pages need more than the pastor as regular guy or gal. They need a shepherd whose care for them arises out of the grace that is first experienced and then mediated in the acts of ministry. Then both people and pastor can live daily in the world with the dignity that comes through well-tested faithfulness. It is the dignity that will finally be restored to the whole creation now groaning in anticipation of the promised day of Christ's return in glory.

4

4

Turning Conflict into Ministry

HE MYTH PERSISTS THAT CHRISTIANS GET ALONG AND THAT
conflict has no place in any congregation living under the
Prince of Peace. When conflicts do appear, as inevitably
is the case, the more common response is denial rather than
forthright attention to the underlying causes. Both the myth and
the response bring problems. The issue is not whether conflict
occurs but of what kind and for what reason.

To be sure, some conflicts come from "stupid, senseless
controversies [that] breed quarrels" (2 Tim. 2:23) in the congregation. That kind of ruckus has no place among those who
would claim to live together under the Savior. Paul's straight
talk to Timothy about what to do when it crops up is but one
of scores of New Testament admonitions for the faithful to
please shut up, shape up, and stop squabbling.

But believers experience another, deeper conflict when
joining God in his saving work in the world. It is unavoidable,
nothing to be ashamed of or surprised by, and a sure badge of
discipleship under Christ. He promised his church that conflict
awaits all who take up their cross and follow him into the daily
life of the world. Living the Good News that Jesus is the crucified Lord, now risen and ruling, collides head-on with a world
that prefers something other than the foolishness of the gospel,
a gospel of which the church dare never be ashamed. Because
of the very nature of the gospel itself, conflict is inevitable, and
its battle line runs through the center of every believer's heart
as well as between the church and the world. Experiencing it is
a sign that the gospel is alive and ever a stumbling block to the
religiously self-righteous, and foolishness to the intellectually

arrogant. *That* conflict, the mark of costly grace clashing with all that cheapens it, is no reason to deny conflict or to accede to any impulse to dodge it. It is written into the very charter of Christ's commissioning of his church as his body in the world. If that means taking our lumps from those who scorn the truth, so be it. Wearing a few battle scars qualifies us for a modest place in the long and noble line of saints and martyrs whose witness is a treasure to cherish rather than an embarrassment to hide.

Conflict resolution in the sense of settling personal or organizational disputes is a virtual growth industry in our time, much of which is necessary and good. What too often hampers effective resolution, however, is an assumption that conflict is a bump in the normally smooth road of human affairs. It is seen as only negative, an aberration from the norm that needs fixing, the sooner the better. Sound pastoral ministry looks deeper, not settling for the quick fix that can mean the loss of salutary lessons learned only through grappling faithfully with problems. Facing and enduring conflict, within the congregation as well as in the congregation's mission to the surrounding community and beyond, means uprooting sin at its core. That hard work of exposing sin is analogous to dying, and repenting, turning life around through forgiveness. Then comes the real resolution of conflict, which means a reconciliation analogous to rising with Christ to fresh beginnings. That is what happens when conflicted Christians return daily to baptism for the grace needed to wage the good fight of faith.

Over and over again through the years I have had to learn the truth that the congregation was a unique place where conflict became an opportunity for ministry. Through the 1960s when America was jolted to the core by the racial conflict, the temptation was strong in our middle- to upper-middle-class congregation to have nothing to do with racial injustice in Chicago and our suburban environs. I confess to duping myself with notions that people had enough to deal with and that the congregation was a safe haven against overload. Later, when the Vietnam War heightened conflict all over the land, the same temptation continued as strident campus protest met the no-less-strident refusal to face the tragic reality of a lost cause. The unspoken mantra was that conflict would just go away if the Silent Majority was silent long enough. Moreover, during those very decades a God-awful denominational conflict engulfed us for 20 years, piling conflict upon conflict. Our congregation and my pastoral ministry had to face them and strive to apply the Word and the sacraments as means of healing. How we did so is detailed in part below and elsewhere in these pages. That sad history has been told elsewhere and sometimes dwelt upon obsessively. The point at hand here is that conflict, when caused by costly discipleship, deepens faith and provides a compelling witness to the world.

I think of conflict in this chapter not only as the church against the world but also as the church at odds with itself. Who among us is not touched in some measure by the high-tension "worship wars" pitting proponents of contemporary worship styles against those who uphold traditional hymnody and liturgy? The conflict over sexual ethics, specifically the ordination of gay clergy and the blessing of same sex-couples, threatens Christian unity on a global scale. The overworked labels of "conservative" and "liberal" in matters ranging from biblical interpretation to church-state relations dominate press coverage, both secular and religious. What is not widely covered, however, is how conflicts are resolved and what is learned in that process. My experience is that we can see ministry at work in conflict more in hindsight than while sweating it out in the trench warfare of protracted battles. If the lessons gained through the conflicts described here offer more than war stories, then the ministry that emerges can be a hopeful sign that the peaceable kingdom keeps on coming among us with healing and reconciling grace.

Anfechtung

Anfechtung: "temptation" is a dictionary translation of this German word for which we have no adequate English equivalent.

Never mind the semantics. It has become an important word in my ministry, and I have some things to say about it.

Anfechtung is not just any kind of temptation. It is the temptation to give up on the power of the gospel to prevail against demonic forces. In my experience, that dark reality was sometimes felt as a heaviness within, a feeling of foreboding coming from something more sinister than human orneriness. It felt like being sucked into a black hole of the spirit, a wearying awareness of evil so palpable that one could almost touch and taste it. Psalm 88 is the lament of one in the grip of *Anfechtung* as the psalmist cries out his feelings of abandonment by God, his sense of forsakenness as evil stalks the land. The deceptive force of this malady of soul is that it empties the gospel of its good news for this painful situation. Satan is at work, not only overtly like a roaring lion destroying by brute force but also more subtly, stirring up bitterness and hate among people who sit in church pews, hear (or preach) sermons, receive the sacrament, and participate in congregations. *Anfechtung* is the temptation to functional atheism, the despair that God is dead, that his Son's body rots in Joseph's tomb, and that the Holy Spirit is nothing but hot air.

Where did I run into *Anfechtung*? Or better, where did it grab me by the throat? In the church. That's the first clue to its deceptive nature, that it slips in under the cover of religion gone disastrously wrong. That can happen on a massive scale, as evidenced by genocidal wars in Rwanda, the former Yugoslavia, and Sudan. It is key to understanding the complexities of the Middle East conflict fueled by Sunni and Shiite factions within Islam. And one need only say the word "crusade" to stir animosities still simmering a thousand years after Christians sought to wrest the Holy Land from Islamic rule by the power of the sword. These instances document the dark powers of evil that bring death and destruction wholesale across the face of the earth,

But the church, the congregation of the faithful, is the setting closer to home where demonic forces seek to seduce and destroy. They don vestments, spout Bible passages, claim unflawed doctrinal purity, and adopt a cloying piety. They are what Paul described in one of the most sobering passages in the New Testament as evil at work among the principalities and powers in heavenly places (Eph. 6:12). To anyone standing in the tradition of Martin Luther, a veteran battler against *Anfechtung* if ever there was one, this all-out attack on the core of the faith should come as no surprise.

Anfectung surely caught me by surprise, however, in its outbreak in our denomination from 1969 until 1985. This was the 16-year span during which Grace Church became a lightning rod for the conflict that literally tore apart the Lutheran Church–Missouri Synod, our denominational home from 1902 until 1977. The battle has spread to other denominations today, as Southern Baptists know all too well. The presenting issue was the doctrine of verbal inspiration of the Bible, with a strong overlay of bad denominational politics that turned church conventions into pitched battles of divisiveness. At the heart of it all was the deeper issue around which *Anfechtung* swirls, the silencing of the gospel, the discounting of Christ's atonement for the forgiveness of the sins of the world as the true treasure of the church, resulting in our failure to love and forbear each other in contending for the faith. Grace Church came directly into the line of fire when gifted parishioners who were on the faculty of nearby Concordia College, an LC–MS institution, were accused by denominational leaders of false doctrine, tried, and deposed from their teaching ministries. To see, hear, feel, and endure what happened to faithful people was to know *Anfechtung* firsthand. For several years we devoted open, well-publicized parish meetings, with several hundred members regularly attending, to issues related to the denominational conflict and its impact on our mission and ministry. For several days before those meetings I would feel it coming on, this shroudlike fog of heaviness of spirit that tempted me to wonder whether the gospel was sufficient to carry us through. I hated those attacks that shook me to my core and hampered my daily work of pastoral ministry. But what heartened me was the presence of the people of Grace, in those meetings but especially in the daily rounds of encountering them in the daily work of ministry—comforting the sick and aged, counseling, preaching, and teaching. The people of the congregation ministered to me. That fog lifted. I was set free for servant leadership, and could leave the outcome of wearisome conflicts to God.

I learned things about ministry amidst *Anfechtung* through those years. One was that parishioners needed some visible target when confused, irked, and upset—and that target sometimes was me. When we withdrew from the denomination and endured a lengthy court battle over ownership of the church property, it was painful to lose some parishioners who left Grace Church. Yet I am grateful for what I learned during ministry through this dark side of pastoral experience. The primary lesson was that Satan is ever the quintessential deceiver. His stranglehold is possible only through the power that is of God but is usurped and misused. *Anfechtung,* which seems so lethal and interminable in an encounter, dissipates and slouches off when faced by the gospel at work in faithful people. This is so because the Holy Spirit who indwells us is one with Jesus Christ, who cried out from the cross to his Father from depths of abandonment beyond our knowing. I would have missed the power and comfort of that costly grace had I sidestepped the controversy with the excuse of protecting the congregation or being too busy with other things. I learned the deeper meaning of what Luther called the theology of the cross, finding in the wounds of Christ the mystery of enduring faith. I learned that theology not from a book but in the bone and marrow of my being. It has carried me through all my subsequent years of pastoral ministry and has given me more patience and perspective on the human side of the church.

Sin

"Don't you know that you don't sin any more after you're 80?" The suggestion ranks well up there on the list of wrongheaded statements I've heard about sin. It came from an octogenarian who was wondering why I was bringing Holy Communion to her next-door neighbor in a nearby retirement home. I didn't stop for debate; the Grace parishioner I was calling on—also an octogenarian—wanted Holy Communion and wasn't about to refuse it on the grounds that she had outlived the need for the forgiveness of her sins.

Confusion about sin, like the poor, is always with us. An abiding source of that confusion is defining sin so narrowly, moralistically, and individualistically that it boils down to sexual temptation, murder, or thievery. To be sure, sin is involved in all three. But sin, the word used in the singular, goes deeper than a particular misdeed. It poses one of the most challenging truths to pastoral ministry that I know of. In its deeper, biblical meaning, sin is not only this or that wrongdoing but our condition of separation from God that underlies it all, the dilemma that besets us from birth. By our nature as children of Adam and Eve, we do not love, honor, and trust God above all things. The Fall did us in. That's our predicament. The Greek New Testament term for "sin," *hamartia,* portrays the whole trajectory of our lives as veering off course. The word for sin pictures an archer, drawing the bow back full length, then releasing the arrow intended for the target—but the arrow goes awry, doing unspeakable damage all around. Moreover, it's not just me as an individual, but the whole of humanity that is off course, needing radical turning around and reconnecting to God.

Whatever Happened to Sin? is the title of a landmark book by psychiatrist Karl Menninger published some decades ago. He puzzled over the church's replacement of the deep biblical understanding of sin with pop therapies that miss real diagnosis. Too often we clergy have ourselves to blame for "whatever happened to sin." That happens when our preaching veers off into providing an entertaining diversion from realities in a fallen world, or moralizing over the latest downfall of someone prominent, or taming biblical texts down by never letting them out of the first century. Settling for pap rather than substance deprives the faithful of the law of God that exposes sin at work in racism, war, corporate greed, or national idolatry. Reinhold Niebuhr and Martin Luther King, Jr., were potent witnesses to God's judgment on sin ingrained in institutional life in America in previous decades. Activist theologian Jim Wallis, in *God's Politics: Why the Right Gets It Wrong and the Left Doesn't Get It* (HarperSanFrancisco, 2005) carries that prophetic theological tradition into our time as he takes on major political and social issues in and beyond America and shows how applying the biblical faith overcomes partisanship and calls the church to wider, deeper service. We may not be gifted for public ministry at the national and global level, but we can discern how sin afflicts and grace renews the lives of those gathered with us week after week as hearers and doers of the Word.

We need only to think, really stop and think, of what we do when we confess our sin, speaking words that are second in importance to no other words spoken anywhere. Confession of sin is *not* about feeling good, *not* about being comfortable. It's hellishly uncomfortable, unless, of course, we're only talking to ourselves. But to stand without pretense before the living God, to confess sin as bondage from which we cannot free ourselves, to say without dissembling that there is no health in us, and to acknowledge responsibility for the terrible damage sin inflicts upon others is nothing less than to die by drowning—to keep the baptismal imagery vivid (Rom. 6:2–4). Yet that is what confession is meant to be—every syllable, word, phrase, and sentence of the confession of sins, totally counter to the blasé dismissal of sin so common in the culture all around us. It is good at times to invite the congregation to a lengthier period than usual for silence in preparing to speak the general confession in the liturgy. It shatters all pride and pretense to tell God the truth about our thoughts, words, and deeds that have caused such offense and damage. When such respect is offered to God, the gates of hell itself are rattled off their hinges. More than we may realize, the liturgical action (liturgy means "work of the people") of confessing sin and embracing forgiveness equips faithful men and women for another week of life in the world as coworkers with God. And that, in turn, means nothing less than partnership with God in dismantling evil where we meet it and joining the Almighty in moving the whole creation closer to its completion in the promised Day of Christ yet to come (Rom. 8:18–25).

Articulating sin, that slippery three-letter word, as it turns up in contemporary life is an ever-daunting challenge. A half-century ago, "living in sin" meant two unmarried people cohabitating under the same roof; today the arrangement is increasingly common without the connotation of missing the mark of God's purpose for marriage. Gambling once conjured the image of backroom crap-shooting; now gambling has been elevated to state-sponsored *wagering* with no hint that sin is involved. Likewise, the *lottery*—state sponsorship for the sin of greed—has arrived at respectability as a game for everybody, an amusing way to feed the illusory odds of winning millions for a dollar ticket.

Persistence in preaching the law and gospel of God, in season and out of season, and doing so with a keen eye for how God's judgment and grace make all the difference in the contemporary human situation, is as great a gift as any a pastor can ask for. *Deo gratias,* we needn't try to do it alone. We are partners with parishioners and ministry colleagues. We're not the first or the last to face this staggering challenge. The sacred Scriptures still deliver truth that finally prevails over all the pretensions of sin. The long, noble line of preachers and martyrs still surrounds us as a great cloud of witnesses, cheering us on as the Hebrews 12:1 passage suggests. In literature, art, drama, music, and poetry, portrayals of sin and grace inspire and inform many whom we may not reach but are reached nonetheless because the Word is not bound. And as we are honest with ourselves, we proclaim and minister knowing that the "axis of evil" is not an arbitrary designation among nations but a line running first and foremost through our own hearts.

I learned plenty about the pervasiveness of sin by paying attention to our life together within the Grace congregation. During my watch we struggled imperfectly with racism, war, anti-Semitism, triumphalism, and scorn for the homeless, to mention some of our encounters with sin embedded in societal institutions. We struggled imperfectly through the conflicts caused by our own pettiness, neglect of each other, insufficient stewardship, and failure to appreciate the astonishing breadth and depth of blessings God had given us. In short, we sinned. We continue to sin. And that's not going to stop. It is not an excuse for cheap grace, as the line often attributed to Heinrich Heine puts it: "I like to sin. God likes to forgive. Really, the world is admirably arranged."

The truth easily overlooked is that as individuals and as a community, we are at one and the same time saint and sinner, forgiven and rebel, saved and still stiff-arming the Spirit. This Jekyll-Hyde truth about us gave me something to say to those from outside Grace Church who sometimes told me about the difference they saw between church people on Sundays and church people during the week. I've heard it all. And my response always surprises: "You don't know the half of it . . . beginning with me." It's not a smart-aleck comeback to what may be an earnest plea for integrity. It's the truth. Our sins, painfully evident to human eyes, are not the half of what God's eyes behold.

But the gospel creates new beginnings despite the wreckage of sin, for God is unconditionally merciful. He reclaims sinners in baptism and continually renews his own who return daily to baptism for what it takes to get on in our calling. Sin doesn't have the last word on us, our congregations, or our world. No wonder, then, turning sin into an occasion for ministry begins at the doorstep of our own hearts each new day with hope for a full and final peace to battles within and without. That promise rests ultimately with the Holy Ghost, who, in one poet's memorable words, "over the bent World broods with warm breast and with ah! bright wings" (Gerard Manley Hopkins, "God's Grandeur," 1877).

Meanness

"There is no lack of meanness in the world. Do we really need to add to it in the church?" As often as I have heard this sentiment expressed, often with a sigh, it rests on the wrong assumption. The church is not the gathering of the elite in whom meanness has no chance. The church is the gathering of the forgiven who in penitence fight meanness wherever it turns up, including the church.

Still, the pain of meanness is even more hurtful when Christians inflict it. Christ is betrayed anew whenever deliberate, bare-knuckled meanness crops up in the congregation, especially under the guise of piety. Jesus's parable of the wicked tenants who killed the heir to the vineyard is one of his sternest parables (Luke 20:9–19), a warning to his followers of that ultimate meanness that would lead finally to the cross. The church, as our Lord above all knows, is not the last but the first place for the Enemy to plant seeds of meanness. How can we surprised by that truth, then, particularly as we take a deeper look into ourselves and the situations in which meanness occurs?

Letters (and now e-mails) written in unholy anger are often the prime bearers of meanness. I've received my share of zingers, most of them concluding with "Yours in Christ," or "With Christian concern," or "Prayerfully yours," and the like. It would have been more honest if the sign-off sentiments were "You're hell-bound, you know," or simply "Get out." My predecessor at Grace told a story of how he once dealt with a poison-pen letter left for him as he arrived for a Christmas Eve service. He read it, conducted the service, and after the benediction asked the congregation to be seated. He then read the letter aloud and stated that if even one person would arise to support its mean-spirited allegations, he would resign then and there. After turning to the altar for silent prayer, he turned to face a congregation with no one standing (or even slunk down under the pew!). He then wished all a happy Christmas celebration in their homes and returned home to one of his own. That audacious moment was a turning point in his first year leading a stormy congregation, and it met a need at that time, but he wisely advised me not to think it could become standard procedure.

Receiving a straightforward shot of meanness is never an easy experience, but it is better than the genre covered over with false piety. I recall once a visitation from three men I had never seen before. They walked into my study, announced their purpose of praying for me to be delivered from alleged false doctrine, got on with their prayer and left abruptly. At least there was no subtlety about that weird visit by a hit squad of self-appointed doctrinal police. I recall the meeting night when the Grace congregation voted to withdraw from membership in the denomination. A woman I had called on for years looked me straight in the eye to say exactly what she felt: "I wish you had never been born." I recall another occasion when a man twisted around like a pretzel in the pew, trying to raise *both hands* to vote against a measure he passionately opposed, an effort that was as funny as it was mean-spirited. One Sunday in my sermon I applied the text of Jesus's rebuke of his disciples, ready to call down fire on the Samaritans, to our government's bombing of innocent civilians. A parishioner immediately arose, tore an offering envelope into small pieces, and stomped out. On another occasion, an all-congregation meeting on a controversial matter, several members arranged for a court reporter to be seated front and center as a mean-spirited effort to intimidate free exchange of viewpoints (it didn't work). My heart grieved for children of unhappy homes who would tell me of promises made to them by an absentee parent that were never kept. They experienced heartbreak through a meanness more shattering than anything I had to cope with in my calling. And other pastors who have weathered meanness in multiple congregations served have much more to say about this subject than I.

I do own up to an unorthodox way of dealing with some instances of over-the-top meanness that occasionally came my way in phone calls intended for sheer spite. Beverly and I received a plaque at a housewarming party of "spoof" gifts shortly after our wedding. In Gothic script, beautifully hand-lettered by a friend, it read, "I had one grunch, but the eggplant over there . . ." and was attributed as "Old Saying." It was literally, of course, nonsense. Sometimes I resorted to quoting it to end noncommunication with crank callers who at all hours were after my jugular vein. I couldn't think of a more benign answer for people high on meanness.

I confess to doing meanness as well as to being done unto. Once, on a chilly, wet night while interning in Japan, I had paused under a dim streetlight to rest a minute while walking my bike up a steep hill. Out of the shadows a young woman appeared, a prostitute with a proposition. Her sad face caked with make-up and her tired smile suggested that perhaps she was new and tentative at the world's oldest profession. In any case, the only answer I could give to her come-on, which left me befuddled as well as a bit fascinated, was the dumb question "How much?" She hesitated, as if searching for an answer that would work, then answered *"Rohbyaku yen"*—600 yen, in those days less than two dollars. With an edge of sarcasm in my voice, I responded, *"Anata yasui desu, neh!"*—"You're really cheap, aren't you?" and got on my bike for the steep climb home. That was a mean slur bathed in self-righteousness, a cruel dig at a fellow human being, so different from Jesus's response offering redeeming tenderness to a woman once taken in adultery (John 8:1–11). I have asked his forgiveness and in receiving it have tried to keep Christ's forbearing love foremost when dealing with meanness in whatever form it has appeared in my ministry. Doing so has helped me better understand meanness, not as a permanent acid that eats up the soul entirely, but as a toxic flare-up of anger that needs attention without allowing the flare-up to define the whole essence of another's being.

In the years of my pastorate at Grace I've learned that people who are hurting may dump their frustrations and resentments on the congregation, somehow sensing that the parish is a safe place to do so. Often the meanness that flares up in a parishioner stems from an anger unconnected to the congregation, but it spills out with unexpected venom and leaves both the offender and the offended surprised and chagrined. Marital problems and family heartaches are prime sources for those festering sores, not to mention long-term frustrations at work. With that background in mind, the pastoral response has to be more than either silence or a judgmental word. It is better to accept an ugly outburst of meanness, irksome as it is, and treat it as a malady from a deeper source that needs healing than to react with anger or neglect. Doing either can set up the conditions for the worst of all outcomes, a hardened heart.

The remedy for meanness in the congregation, valid in the church for all time, comes from a veteran who knew it firsthand:

> Put away from you all bitterness and wrath and anger and wrangling and slander, together with all malice, and be kind to one another, tenderhearted, forgiving one another, as God in Christ has forgiven you.
>
> Ephesians 4:31–32

Anger

I count Stephen as a very close friend and a brother in the faith. The feeling is mutual. It wasn't that way, however, prior to an angry blowup that cleared the air between us, allowing us to reach a far more honest, healthy friendship.

The particular conflict that triggered the explosion of anger isn't the point. We all have them. The point is that anger had been allowed to fester much too long. Steve was nettling me, I felt, and no doubt he felt the same vibes continually coming from me.

Finally—I think because of a letter he wrote me—I let the long-brewing anger inside me boil over. I recall sitting down at the typewriter and pounding so hard that I nearly broke the keyboard. Then, against all better judgment, I mailed him the letter.

That evening the sun went down, of course. But a sentence of Paul's would not let go of me: "Be angry but do not sin; do not let the sun go down on your anger, and do not make room for the devil" (Eph. 4:26–27). First off the next morning I wrote another letter to Stephen with these opening words: "The storm has passed . . ." I was free to speak my regret for the damage my anger had done to him, along with the hope that we could both see what the other felt and stood for and then take each other with new seriousness. That's why the emotion of anger had to get out of the basement lockup and be exposed to the fresh air of honest give-and-take. Letting the sun set many times without getting anger out into the open is storing up rage. It will surely eat away with its toxic effect at everything we are as people with feelings and body, mind and spirit.

Stephen accepted me, warts and all, an act for which I am grateful. It is peevish, not righteous, anger that is sinful. The latter is a galvanizing emotion that gets us to do the necessary deed rather than procrastinate. Sin gets an opening when anger is kept inside, nursed to fester into seething resentment that can seduce pastor and people into thinking we are above anger, never vexed, perpetually cool, serenely turning the other cheek, self-righteous in fact, and all the while self-deceived into think-ing that ice water, not warm blood, flows through our veins. Did not our Lord himself upend the tables of the money changers in the temple, surely red-faced with righteous anger when he did so? If he could vent such a powerful emotion, then all of us who bear his name can learn to do the same and follow it with the will to reconcile and move on.

Living under the forgiving Christ, Stephen and I learned to work together in numerous ways in the parish, mostly agreeing, sometimes differing, but no longer imprisoned by a seething rancor toward each other. My eyes have been opened to his many gifts that bless me and many others. We could laugh, think, pray, talk, argue, console, work, and enjoy friendship together. When we needed to, we could embrace as a sign of the peace that keeps us. In my final meeting with the board of elders before retirement, his eloquent words spoken to me are a permanent treasure. They were, to quote John Henry Newman's motto, *cor ad cor loquitur,* heart speaking to heart. We put Christ-given love that saves us from ourselves into the service of fruitfully working together for others.

The old typewriter that took such a pounding is long gone. The anger, too.

Failure

"I'm here to tell you how you've failed me as a pastor." That's how he opened the conversation in my study, this man who came to tell me exactly how he saw me and my calling at Grace Church. His declaration got my attention, at least, and we were into what was a difficult but important exchange. I knew the man who spoke it, not well, but well enough not to be either surprised or offended by his straightforward listing of where I had failed him: my preaching (too ecumenical), pastoral prefer-ences (his child's baptism was celebrated in the Sunday service rather than privately at home), and social ministry (too close to home for comfort). Just by listening instead of interrupting him with rebuttal, I gained a new insight into this capable, professionally successful man. He got around to reflecting upon the fact that his real problem was with authority and a kind of love/hate relationship with it going back to his father, who always had to have the final say-so about everything. That made me wonder whether the real agenda had shifted from what he perceived as my failures to unresolved issues with his father.

But in ways he was undoubtedly unaware of, he spoke for others who for whatever reason never got around to talking to me about failures in my ministry that I should have recognized and corrected. Grace parishioners were far more generous with kudos than with criticism through the years. An unintended seduction lies hidden in that graciousness, however. It fosters the idea that pastoral ministry thrives on success and that call-ing the pastor to task for failure is bad manners. This attitude is strange. We all claim allegiance to biblical truth. Yet we seem to miss the point that Scripture is unsparing when revealing the failures of men and women, great and small, who are presented in its salvation history. Of course! They lived by the salvation that was divine grace for otherwise failed lives.

I have committed some failures that were lulus. It was not calamitous that I totally forgot Mabel and Walter Pitann's golden wedding celebration, but it was embarrassing for me to own up to it with apologies for having missed it cold. I did remember to officiate at the golden wedding anniversary service and party for another couple, and to take part in the festivities that followed. But toward the end of the reception for Fred and Edna Iwert, upon whom I had heaped praise in my pastoral remarks, she leaned over to me and gently reminded me that her name is Edna, not Edith.

I've known failures that turned out to have more positive than negative results. I did not pass the field examination, the last step before dissertation writing in the doctoral program at the University of Chicago. Fortunately, neither did I flunk it beyond repair. The committee gave me the opportunity to redo the oral segment of the exam several months later. The second try was a far more purposeful learning experience, having to do with organizing and thinking more clearly under pressure.

I've experienced failures that were turning points. Returning from two years of internship in Japan for my final year of theology in St. Louis, I had a strong urge to study medicine after seminary toward a future medical-missionary vocation. I made an appointment with the medical school dean at nearby Washington University. When he learned that I was in my final year at Concordia Seminary, he brought the interview to an abrupt end, declaring that medical-school academic requirements were well beyond the ability of theological students. Thus ended my brief exploration of medical missions. I failed before even getting to the starting line. As irked as I was by the arrogance of the dean, I have not lost sleep over that failure. It was the kind of turning point that confirmed my vocational direction.

I recall a failure on a fairly large scale that now seems wonderful in ways I could not grasp at the time. Fellow pastor Bertwin Frey and I mounted a denomination-wide movement to counterbalance what we perceived to be a stifling dogmatic legalism that was silencing the gospel. The effort took up plenty of time and energy for a half-dozen years, and in church political terms, the Frey/Lueking effort was a smashing failure. We were creamed, particularly in a denominational convention that soundly voted down all we stood for and voted out nearly all the leaders who had served the Lord faithfully. It took a while to see the failure for what it was—a clearing of the decks that made room for new things to happen. That failure within the church body left Grace Church free to serve in new ways. Through the trouncing also emerged the leaven of faculty, clergy, and congregations that left the denomination to enrich a new body of Lutherans a few years later, the Evangelical Lutheran Church in America. Such a failure, painful though it was, was part of the wisdom of God's ways once stated by the eminent biblical scholar Walter Brueggemann: "The future for which you are so intensely striving is passing away." That prophetic insight fit our situation of failure, which turned into something beyond our expectations.

I have known times when, going home from a Sunday service, I have felt that the sermon preached was not effective, only to have some person mention weeks or months later that the Word preached that day reached a need about which I knew nothing. The opposite is no less true. At times when I felt the preaching was right on, it wasn't.

At the very heart of the Christian gospel, and thus at the core of the pastoral calling to proclaim it, is the most monumental failure of all: the human failure to measure up to the righteousness of God. That failure has been conquered by the cross and resurrection of Jesus Christ our Lord.

With that huge, damning failure out of the way, why think that all lesser failures must obsess us? The sentence of acquittal God himself has pronounced upon us continually sets us free to face failure, learn from it, marvel that it no longer controls us, bear with others who also know failure, and move on with deepened maturity through the grace of God who makes all things new.

The Four-Minute Rule

The Four-Minute Rule states that on any given day, only four minutes may be spent talking about a problem that would otherwise eat up too much of the day. I recommend it highly for anybody.

When our congregation-denomination collision became more than a passing brouhaha, my own involvement in the issues increased. The mess had the potential to eat me up, inside and out. Throughout those years, I kept close contact with a close friend. Among our times of respite were regular evenings enjoying supper and Chicago Symphony concerts, impromptu picnics with our families at a nearby forest preserve, and holiday dinners together. On those happy occasions, the temptation was to turn to "The Controversy," but our spouses and children helped us put a lid on our letting it dominate. Thus the Four-Minute Rule was born.

Sometimes the time limit was stretched to five. On rare occasions we managed to hold problem matters to less than four minutes. The point was to set a conscious limit on the time we would give it. Ending the conversation didn't mean we stopped thinking about it. But it did prevent our being swallowed up by the problem, to the relief of our families and friends as well as to our own good. I can remember coming home from a particularly stressful day of hate mail or ugly phone calls, entering the house, pouring it all out to Beverly (always away from the hearing of the children), and then hearing the ding-ding-ding of the kitchen timer she had set at four minutes as soon as I walked in. I had to change the subject. The rule worked. It freed me to begin asking Beverly how her day went, what mail arrived, how the Chicago Cubs were doing, what was for supper, and other matters that helped me avoid becoming stuck on one note.

Looking back, I have an extra reason to be grateful for the ongoing use of the Four-Minute Rule in later times of turbulence. I know it helped keep my blood pressure low and my mien a good deal more bearable. I had friends in ministry who were eaten up by the acidity of church fights and who left the ministry embittered and broken. I knew several who died too early from causes I have to believe were not unrelated to the stress they suffered.

The Four-Minute Rule denies worry its potency. Furthermore, it is a healthy preventive against terminal boredom inflicted on those who have to listen.

Regret

"Any regrets?" was TV host Larry King's question to a celebrity looking back over his years of notoriety. "None whatsoever!" was the quick response, a little too quick it seemed to me, and an answer that made me wonder. At the other end of the spectrum is "If only . . . ," implying nothing but gloom seen when looking back. We get a hint of that gloom in Luke's account of the disciples walking to Emmaus that first Easter afternoon, with their "we had hoped" sentence of regret spoken to the risen Companion they did not recognize. Between airheadedness and despondency there is surely a place for healthy regret, to learn from it, to pass it on to others for their good.

Regrets can be recalled as the years lengthen, not to despair but to clarify what was once confused. I see regret as another side of penitence when we learn from sins of commission and omission and gain maturity through the grace that covers them. So, let me speak of regrets that stay with me on my journey in hope that such memories can help.

In looking back over my Grace years, I regret not encouraging more young people to become pastors and teachers in the church. Our congregation overflowed with gifted people of all ages. I wish that I could have found ways to stimulate them to consider the pastoral ministry, as well as other forms of church work. But my mind is particularly on the pastoral office. There is already a shortage of seminary candidates of sound quality. Who will serve the spiritual good of our grandchildren and their children? I regret not mentoring more men and women toward such a future.

I regret waiting too long to spend more time with youth and children, to include them more effectively in worship, preaching, and other aspects of parish life. I showed up too rarely at their school events, sports, music, drama, graduation, and other opportunities to learn more about their world. I regret not making youth ministry a higher priority. Specifically, I regret not continuing my earlier hands-on pastoral leadership in preparing 10-year-olds for communion and older children for confirmation. I'm grateful for a widened team of staff helpers in both groups and honor their effectiveness. But if I had it to do it all again, I would spend more time closer to children learning the basics of the faith.

I regret not clearing out more quiet time for keener listening and responding to God in prayer. I could begin and end the day with petitions of thanksgiving and intercessions for others, but I did not enter into the discipline of more time set aside at other times of the day for opening my mind and heart to God. As one too busy with too many things at the expense of the one thing needful, I have been more Martha than Mary, according to the story in Luke 10:38–42 that has always come to my ears as needed judgment. I am grateful for much gained from the African Christians with whom I have been associated in continuing ministries after retiring from Grace. Their days are no less full than mine, yet their example of rising early for prayer and Scripture reading encourages me to follow their example.

I regret not making a stronger effort to build bridges between separated Christians in general and Lutherans in particular. My efforts to relate to clergy on the far right and left were too sporadic. Several times I attended prayer and study groups in which I felt an uneasy welcome, but those efforts on my part were too short-lived. When Grace left our former denomination rather than keep fighting within, we did establish new contacts with the ELCA while retaining whatever contacts we could with LC–MS congregations. Among the Grace members, it was Charlotte Scott in particular who kept asking how Grace might somehow be a bridge over the widening gap between the two church bodies. Our geography surely hints at that potential role. We are located on one corner of Concordia University, an important institution of the Lutheran Church–Missouri Synod, and within 20 minutes of the ELCA headquarters. I regret putting Charlotte's proper concern on the back burner for lack of will power and know-how.

I regret my failure to follow up with people who have drifted out of sight. Backdoor losses are not statistics but people who

have dropped away from worship and congregational connection. "Backdoor" as a term doesn't take into account the far
more serious issue, the loss of faith itself. I regret insufficient
prayer for these men and women who could teach us much
about why and how disengagement occurs, especially in our
large and diverse parish. At times I have been brought up short
by a letter or phone call from someone who told me bluntly
their impression that we were more interested in their financial
support than in their lives. In response, I regret not being a
better listener before calling people to their responsibilities of
discipleship under Christ the Lord. Finally, of course, it is always
Christ-given love that must show through in deeds as well as
words. I wish I had shown the patience to outwait and outwit
whatever kept wanderers from returning home.

I regret not reading more. My habit is to put most of it
off until bedtime, which often has meant falling asleep within
minutes with a book or magazine on my chest. I regret not
playing a single game of golf during the past dozen years of
membership in one of our area's golf clubs. (At tennis, which
Beverly and I can play together, I've done better.) While I'm
at it, I regret not learning more Slovak while in Slovakia, not
asking older parishioners to tell me more about our early congregational history, and not asking my paternal grandparents
about the drama of their emigration from Germany to the
Nebraska prairie in the 1880s.

In speaking up about regrets, I run the risk of exposing my
biases at the expense of other blind spots altogether. Be that
as it may, I offer these incomplete jottings as hints for future
agenda-makers at Grace and all congregations to consider. That
may be presumptuous; their hands will be full enough without
my suggestions. The best thing to do with regrets is to offer
them to God, who works good in all things, and whose merciful
forgiveness is my lasting hope and comfort. And for me, maybe
another thing I can do is to look around for that long-neglected
five iron, wherever I last left it.

Turning conflicts, and all that comes with them, into ministry seems a remote possibility, if not impossible, when caught

up within them. When long-term conflicts never become occasions for ministry, pastoral burnout is too often the result. Handling them alone has the same potential. What I want to hand on is a half-century witness to ministry marked by some conflicts, yes, but filled with confidence that the grace of God has been more than sufficient to turn all these things into ministry. Ministry and conflict are not mutually exclusive when one lives through them humbly and honestly, not alone but with others, not obsessively but with the discipline that arises freely as a gift of the Spirit. We learn that they go together in ways we can see sometimes clearly, more often through a glass darkly as God leads his people through, not around, hard things. Paul has a word for us of abiding importance. He spoke hard-earned wisdom when testifying that doors of opportunity for ministry open up but not without obstacles that can be overcome only by passing through them. (1 Cor. 16:9).

5

~

Pastoral Rhythms

A WELCOME RHYTHM MOVES THROUGH THE FLOW OF EVENTS in parish life, giving it shape, variety, and interest. Those who follow the liturgical calendar value the sameness in the cycle of the liturgical seasons that return unchanged year after year. Advent combines themes of judgment and eschatological hope. Christmas celebrates the incarnation of the divine Word, followed by Epiphany with its call to proclaim the light of the Savior to the nations. Lent is the season to lift high the cross, culminating in Holy Week and the three great days of Jesus's passion and death. Easter—where would we be without Easter!—extends the celebration of Christ's resurrection over seven weeks, culminating in the Lord's ascension. Pentecost celebrates the coming of the Holy Spirit; the half year of Sundays following explores how the Spirit indwells the church, culminating in Christ the King Sunday, which ends the church year on a note in sharp contrast to the frenzy of Christmas commercialization, already well begun. Then the whole cycle starts again, spreading the preaching and teaching of the faith across the great salvation history that is the rock upon which the church stands. The rhythm of the church year stretches preaching and worship beyond favorite texts and best-known hymns. Biblical truths too often ignored get a needed hearing. Since the human condition is constantly shifting and varied, faithful proclamation of God's judgment and mercy is never out of date. The traditions of nonliturgical denominations, too, have ways to keep the flow of faith's message moving through the life of the congregation. Festival high points recur annually. Weeks without festivals come and go without particular mountaintop events to set them apart. In both liturgical and nonliturgical traditions, the ordinary and the extraordinary are connected. Each serves the other.

That rhythm brings God's people together for Sabbath worship and sends them out refreshed and equipped by the Word for discipleship in the daily life of the world between Sundays. There is a rhythm to worship that does not require reinvention each week or season. It is a gift. That rhythm has been enriched through the centuries of the church's history by sermons, writings, hymns, prayers, and practices handed down to us in our time.

This rhythmic flow has particular meaning for the pastoral ministry. The topics of this chapter explore aspects of our pastoral calling that both gain from and contribute to the pattern of how ministry is organized. Some are more prominent than others, and there may be a surprise in one or another of the topics selected.

I could not have written this chapter earlier in my ministry. I offer it in gratitude for the privilege of experiencing the rich flow of events in the half-century since my ordination. As I do so I cannot help but realize how much things have changed, yet how much of the basic rhythms of pastoral work remain the same.

Everydayness

Everydayness is a word for something both wonderful and humdrum in our calling. It is one of the least-described aspects of the pastoral life, perhaps because it consists of ordinary things that make up the majority of working hours. I think of such things as answering letters, returning phone calls, keeping an efficient filing system, attending meetings, preparing sermons, teaching confirmands, making pastoral calls on the sick and shut-in, organizing evangelism, providing reports, keeping an eye on finances, knowing what's going on with building maintenance and repair, and last but by no means least, making time for family and friends. Everydayness means routine, which means duties can become tedious and hand-over-hand. But everydayness also means openness to surprises of grace that come in the midst of things routine, always welcome as part of the rhythm of what can turn up in any given day. Above all, everydayness means attentiveness to people and their importance as the quotidian rounds of parish life unfold.

Schedules are essential to everydayness. For congregations with standing committees, the week falls into a pattern of meetings devoted to administration, stewardship, outreach, music, education, spiritual care, and the like. For congregations that operate around parish objectives in which all participate, organizing is still required. Schedules must be set. Pastoral involvement has to be established. Amidst all the diversity of what happens on Sundays and the days between, the routine of everydayness is inevitable.

Every pastor has a unique pattern for getting things done. But how many of us see the importance of steadiness and commitment in the commonplaces connected to all else we do? Solid Sunday preaching requires sound weekday preparation in textual study, thinking through applications to parish life, working hard to eliminate the irrelevant and the obvious in proclaiming the Good News. Effective Christian education at all levels benefits from pastoral input during sometimes tedious planning sessions. Meeting high stewardship goals calls for rightful celebration; it doesn't happen unless preceded by persistence in the long-term task of motivating for faithful giving. Is it because we dote on the extraordinary that we miss the significance of the ordinary, routine moments essential to reaching the high moments of accomplishment? I think so. But since people are involved in the rhythms of parish life, doing well in whatever we do takes in little as well as great things.

We have no choice but to live with everydayness. Living any other way would drive us out of our minds. We can't make nonstop hilltop events the norm, a lesson Peter had to learn after proposing booths to make permanent the glory of the transfigured Jesus (Luke 9:26–38). Jesus said no and led him and the other two disciples down the mountain to resume the duties and demands of the daily rounds. Jesus, the Word made flesh, dwelt among us and hallowed the commonplaces of life. He grew up in the household of Mary and Joseph, visited the temple in his 12th year, called the Twelve from their fishing nets and tax-collection tables, attended the wedding at Cana, met the Samaritan woman at the town well, and so on through his ministry. It was in the setting of everydayness that the reign of God broke in among us. We who serve in Christ's name have little reason either to complain about the daily routine or to miss its meaning.

Doing the more routine work of daily pastoral ministry calls for care in avoiding ruts of carelessness and neglect of people. Allowing that to happen is an inexcusable blight on our calling. Examples come to mind. Failing to return phone calls with reasonable promptness tells callers they don't count. Indifferent pastoral participation in parish meetings robs those who volunteer their time and effort of needed morale and wider ideas. Or routine can suffer from absentmindedness. I can recall an experience of nearly missing a morning meeting with fellow clergy because I was distracted by other demands at the time. Getting there anyway turned out to be more important than I ever dreamed; one of our colleagues came a bit late, ashen-faced and deep in shock from news just received of the death of his physician son. What had been routine was suddenly anything but, and I am grateful that distraction did not keep me from being where I was scheduled to be. We can be grateful that lesser reasons than calamity call us to show up where our attendance is needed. Steadiness in attending to mundane matters comes from valuing people and serving them for their intrinsic worth in the work God gives us to do together.

In ministry amidst mundane circumstances it helps to grow the art of finding people interesting, appearances notwithstanding. That art grows and deepens, I find, by such simple things as occasionally picking up on what seems trite but turns out to be otherwise. Not long ago my wife and I were relaxing after lunch in a guest house where we were lodged for several days.

Beverly was knitting while I was talking with several other guests; all of us were there with world mission interests. From the other side of the room a quiet, diminutive woman saw my wife knitting and came over to see better what she was doing. As the two women began to talk about knitting, it turned out that this slight, reserved woman, walking gingerly because of back problems, was home after devoting 36 years of her life as a Bible translator in the highlands of Papua New Guinea. She had rendered into writing a previously unwritten language, a task of monumental requirements in listening, imagining, and creating. Then she had translated major sections of the Bible into the tribal language of that area. With a little encouragement from Beverly, she unfolded fascinating stories of living alone among people she learned to love and from whom she gained acceptance. She told of walking six hours to the nearest mission station (eight hours returning on the uphill path) for supplies each month and the satisfaction she found in reaching people with the Word in words they could understand. All those amazing details came out of a conversation begun about knitting on a day and at a place that was no more, no less, than routine.

As if that were not enough for one day of finding the extraordinary amidst the ordinary, one of the people with whom I was chatting while Beverly was hearing missionary-linguist stories informed me of an event later that day that we should not miss. The invitation was to attend a Sunday evening Thomas Mass service, something altogether new to me. We entered a huge downtown church (in Helsinki, Finland) at around 4:30. It was empty except for a handful of worshipers who had preceded us. After our host took us to another room of the church to brief us on the origins of the Thomas Mass, a creative venture in liturgical evangelism to young Finnish urbanites disaffected with church and religion, we returned to the sanctuary to find it nearly filled with 800 people and more coming through the doors. The next two hours were a memorable experience in the vitality of an evangelism based in reviving, not disbanding, the liturgical tradition, offered in creative ways that brought disaffected Christians together for worship week after week. Again, all this came from a routine conversation in a guest house, an example of everydayness disclosing the unexpected amid the routine.

The point is not that the spectacular must always follow close upon the mundane in some faraway city. People count whoever and wherever they are. There is an art to discovering their intrinsic worth. It can emerge amidst the rhythms of a congregational event as seemingly uneventful as a church supper. I have a friend who has a feel for the right moment to ask a lesser-known person at the table, "Tell me three things about you that help us know you better." And I've seen something marvelous happen. A person asked such a question is taken by others around the table with a new seriousness, and the conversation engages everyone in discovering things in others they never dreamed. That's part of the art of making ordinary settings count for discovering the worth God has given every person. It is an asset in pastoral ministry, particularly to those who are never asked questions about themselves because they are rarely even noticed.

I regret not having kept a daily journal of the people and events of previous years. My pocket appointment book is the closest I have come. Its pages are full of names and appointments from the daily rounds. But without a smidgen of descriptive comment on people and events, their meaning is now mostly lost. I admire those who keep a better record of daily events. They will come to my time in life with a richer storehouse of memories of parish rhythms and how the ordinary and extraordinary have joined in making the daily rounds memorable.

But whether one keeps a journal or not, it seems to me that if the person phoning in, or sending e-mail, or walking through the door is received as a human being with unique qualities of mind and heart, then everydayness should not deteriorate into tedium or a kind of bored sterility in parish ministry. The work itself, with its rhythms of surprise sustained through sameness of schedule, keeps one interested and interesting. To be sure, the stretches of time when little of note seems to happen can be lengthy and taxing. Teaching confirmands can test pastoral ingenuity, as it should. Older adults can be tedious. And needy people can test pastoral patience. But these things are part of everydayness in ministry and cannot be resented or neglected because they exist. And lest we forget the blessing of being able to get out of bed and put one foot down after the other for another day, there are wake-ups to what can turn up amidst routine.

I recall a walk back to church one day after lunch at home (I must be among the one-tenth of 1 percent of Americans who could walk to and from the same workplace for over four decades), a routine exercise I always enjoyed. When passing one home I heard someone crying from inside an open window. I stopped to inquire if I could help in any way and learned from the mother in the household that her daughter was having a particularly bad day. The daughter was now in her late 40s, her brain badly injured from loss of oxygen, owing to an equipment breakdown when the mother was giving birth. There was nothing more I could do at that moment than listen to a mother's story. But it made me ponder that I was able to get out of bed that morning. This daughter could not. It also brought to mind what it must mean to be a mother and caregiver to a mentally handicapped daughter for more than 40 years. What do I know about tedium and the demands of long-term care, compared to the two women of this household? That encounter did not end with a routine walk back to church. The mother called me after some weeks to ask for ideas about residential care for her daughter after she herself could no longer provide it. Sending that information to her began a ministry through friendship that continued throughout my remaining years at Grace and thereafter. The arrival of Christmas in the ordered rhythm of the church year helps me remember to leave a bottle of champagne at the door and greet a mother whose extraordinary care for her daughter I stumbled across one day in an everyday moment of a routine walk to work.

There is a biblical perspective on everydayness. Psalm 121 concludes with a brief phrase easy to overlook. The psalmist speaks of God's promise to "keep your going out and your coming in from this time on and forevermore" (v. 8). Your going out and your coming in—there it is: *everydayness!*

Doing the Next Thing

Pastors, like people in other walks of life, know times when some besetting problem hangs on and on. We find ourselves like Joe Btfsplk, the Li'l Abner cartoon character who goes nowhere without that dark cloud hovering over his head. The contrary parishioner, the unmet budget, the question of our own adequacy can make a Joe Btfsplk of us. We become preoccupied with the desire to get rid of the cloud and move on. But when demands are tough and confusing, a saving grace emerges, hidden under a prosaic form, doing the next thing.

I speak to this problem from pastoral experiences of discovering this grace amidst long-term dilemmas that didn't go away easily. Conflict between our congregation and the denominational body dragged on for some 15 years. Working through wrinkled staff relationships was another bummer, as was the late-in-the-fiscal-year pressure to meet the parish budget. These and other macro-challenges could have blurred my focus on people in day-to-day ministry. I could not begin to count the times when my complaining mind would ask, "When *will* this ever end?" Then the phone would ring with word of someone taken to the hospital, someone needing pastoral counsel, someone wanting to arrange a wedding. Or a youngster would knock at my study door with the latest riddle. Or a colleague would bring news of something great going on in ministry. Or a homeless person would ask for help. Or Beverly would call to say a friend would be with us at our supper table. Such things would yank me back to the reality that something and not nothing can be done—the next thing. And in the course of doing the next thing, the cloud that seemed so overshadowing would back off. I was not as stuck as I thought.

Something I rarely thought about was the fact that people coming in for help were themselves doing the only thing they could do in their dilemma—the next thing. In such moments I was called upon to be the doer of the next thing, being faithful in little things, as our Lord said, before helping them see the bigger task yet to be done.

I have a memory of doing the next thing when thoroughly befuddled by my own mistake one morning at Chicago's O'Hare Airport. Beverly and I arrived in good time for our flight, excited to begin a trip to the Chinese University of Hong Kong for a short-term teaching assignment. After checking in and proceeding to our departure gate, I wrote a few postcards and dropped them into the airport mailbox. When our flight was called, I reached into my sport-coat pocket for the tickets. Empty pocket. Tickets in the mailbox—with the postcards. Momentary paralysis of mind, accompanied by a frozen "Now what?" The next thing to do was dictated by the departure-gate agent in no uncertain terms: "Run, don't walk, *run* back to the check-in counter and buy a new ticket." *Running* as the next thing to do worked. I got the ticket, made the plane, and spent some time on the long ride across the Pacific thinking about separating airline tickets from postcards as the next thing I must do. The experience can serve as a comment on things more commonly known to all in ministry when overwhelmed by the prospect of Holy Week, or the cycle of Christmas services, or when facing up to a parish crisis that has suddenly erupted. Or it might not be something of that order. It might be the mini-panic when losing a point while preaching a sermon, or entering a meeting with news of being one of the speakers—whom the program committee failed to inform. Whatever the occasion, calamitous or not, one can benefit from the "Do the Next Thing" regimen when the pressure is on.

I think of a late-evening call from a parishioner, a bride of less than a year. She had received a phone call from a state trooper a thousand miles away reporting that her husband had been involved in a serous car accident. She was pale with shock when I arrived; it was as though the ominous news sucked all sense about what to do out of the room, and the feeling of helplessness was heavy on all of us. The first thing to do was listen. Then what? Express concern, to be sure, and offer a brief prayer for enough calm in our distraught hearts to allow us to think. Then came, one after another, the sequence of next things to be done. Long-distance phone calls had to be made to try to learn whether her young husband was alive or dead. Then came listening to anguished scenarios about what may have happened—listening without affirming or negating, since I had no idea what had happened, but listening nonetheless. Then came Psalm 130 and Romans 8 to give us ground to stand on. Then came hours of waiting with the young wife and family, hoping for the best and fearing the worst. And when the worst was learned—that this splendid young husband had died in the emergency room of a distant hospital—then came joining the family in grief. The next thing to do was to embrace them, just hold them close as the tears flowed, and then stand back in respectful silence as the bride-turned-widow sat for a long time with her head in her hands.

She then raised her head, looked at me, and asked: What was the next thing to do? It was calling the funeral director she requested, to inform him of the death and to learn the proto-col for returning her husband's body from the distant hospital where he had died. She asked about funeral arrangements at Grace Church, not believing her own voice that such words had to be spoken, such plans had to be made. I assured her that all this could be arranged in due time, after she and the family had had more time to accept what had happened. Throughout these nightmarish hours, my pastoral ministry consisted of be-ing present, remaining silent when that was called for, speaking as needed. Years later now, the widow and family remember hardly any of that. They were too numb to remember, or even to realize at the time, what had to be done. Doing the Next Thing supplied the dots between the blank spaces in mind and heart. Ministering amidst such heartbreak is a sacred privilege and is the first step on the long journey of healing.

After the funeral, during the time when this young widow was recovering from the immediate shock of her loss, came important follow-up pastoral ministry with new ways of doing the next thing. When she was ready, it included putting her in contact with other widows who had wisdom about working through the welter of insurance claims, bank adjustments, changing the will, and the myriad new responsibilities suddenly thrust upon her. That was penultimately useful. But as she later told me, nothing that pastoral and congregational care could do for her compared with the healing power of worshiping with the congregation. The liturgy—offering Christ through the Word preached and the sacrament received, linking her in fellowship with the faithful of all the ages in hymns, prayers, and creed—gave her healing beyond all else. The liturgy, meaning "the work of the people," was for her what it is for countless others, a framework within which people encourage each other through the words of comfort and hope in so many of the hymn verses. The Eucharist enables those communing mutually to "proclaim the Lord's death until he comes" and draw together from the benefits of Christ's passion. Hearing one's own name lifted up in prayer is part of the unique "work of the people" that happens nowhere else. More than we realize, this action of the liturgy is doing the next thing that is sorely needed and deeply nurturing for grieving people.

Doing the Next Thing is woven into the fabric of the grand salvation story. Mary and Joseph journeyed to Bethlehem because of tax-registration requirements. The grateful leper healed by Jesus showed himself to the priest. The paralytic's helpers in Capernaum cleared an opening in the roof to lower him into Christ's presence. The good Samaritan left payment for the poor fellow hijacked on the Jericho road. Simon of Cyrene became the unwitting cross-bearer, his obedience to doing his next thing forever enshrined in the story of Jesus's passion and death. The women at the empty tomb, numb with grief, brought embalming spices, their next thing to do. And now that Christ is indeed risen, we Do the Next Thing in ministry in his name. Amazing and wonderful!

Sabbatical

A sabbatical is good for every pastor and should not be limited to those serving tall-steeple parishes. It is a benison of great promise for clergy serving in parishes of all sizes and circumstances. It is still too rare because of mistaken notions about what it is and who gains from it. These need correcting.

It's not a vacation, nor continuing education in the usual sense of more classroom time, though academics may be involved. It's not time out *from* ministry, but time away *for* ministry. In my case a pastoral sabbatical meant going away from the parish for a specific time and objective. The purpose was to come back refreshed and renewed in ministry with the congregation through the expanded pastoral vision gained on a visit to Christian work around the world. It required careful planning. It didn't happen without my efforts, combined with the support of the congregation that made it happen. That meant envisioning, proposing, presenting, educating, funding, and demonstrating the gain for both people and pastor. Sabbaticals need not be confined to the seven-year cycle, common to academia. Nor should funding put undue financial pressure on the congregation.

My opportunity to initiate the sabbatical idea came when hosting Bernice Feicht for a luncheon several months after the death of her husband. Bernice was the first female stockbroker on the Chicago Board of Trade and excelled as a pioneer in a male-dominated business. She had met her husband, also a competent Chicago BOT veteran, in midlife. Together they did well, very well, financially. But Bernice knew how to give away as well as gather in. This grace opened her to consider a memorial commensurate with her stewardship capacities, and she heard me out on my idea of a pastoral sabbatical fund in Arthur's memory. This was in the late 1970s, when I had already been serving Grace 25 years. During the previous decade I had helped establish two funds for global travel and continuing education for Grace School teachers, the William Garbers Fund and the Bee Johnson Fund. I felt the time was ripe for a fund to support expanded pastoral vision through a sabbatical and to that end outlined a prospectus for the Arthur Feicht Memorial Fund.

Her response was vintage Bernice. She trumped my idea of a substantial interest-bearing fund with her better idea of beginning with a smaller amount to try out the sabbatical idea, evaluate the results, and if the enterprise proved worthy, then adding annual contributions to bring the fund to the level needed. All this with the approval of Grace Church, of course.

As I recall, the pastoral sabbatical was not the only suggestion I offered that day. I invited her to think of other ideas as well. Much to my delight, the sabbatical won out. She pledged the amount needed for the trial run. The elders (whom the memorial fund document named as supervisors of the sabbatical), the church council, and the congregation all agreed. We spent about a year educating the congregation to the idea and refining the administrative details. Any shortcuts would not have helped, since the concept of a pastoral sabbatical was new at Grace, and we had few models from which to learn.

The activity I chose for my first sabbatical was to get a firsthand look at a profound shift in global Christianity during the middle decades of the 20th century. The center of Christian expansion was no longer western Europe and North America but new centers where I wanted to go to learn: sub-Saharan Africa, Southeast Asia, South Korea, and mainland China. From the apostolic era when Paul responded to the cry, "Come over to Macedonia and help us!" (Acts 16:9), the expansion of Christianity had been primarily westward. In the middle of the 20th century a sea change occurred. How and why did this happen? What could it mean for our part of the world, our congregation?

This sabbatical focus grew out of a conversation early in the 1980s when Grace collegian Andrew Miller and his parents, Clark and Marion, were our Sunday dinner guests. Like so many serendipitous nudgings of the Holy Spirit, listening to Andrew describe his teaching experience in a *harambe* (Swahili for "let's all pull together") high school in a remote region of western Kenya gave me the spark of an idea with a future. As a junior at Davison College in North Carolina, Andrew had taken a year for study in Kenya and was already on his way toward a career in America/Africa bridge-building that has continued into his present faculty role in African studies at the University of Michigan.

Much planning followed that Sunday dinner. I wrote to people I knew in Europe, Israel, Kenya, India, Nepal, Thailand, Hong Kong, China, South Korea, and Japan, asking for help in understanding church life in their context. In every case, I came with a simple question: what is it like to be a Christian where you live and serve? By visiting congregations with this inquiry in mind, staying for varying lengths of time in varying places (including a month in Kenya), I hoped to discern something, at least, of how the gospel was faring in primarily Third World places, what obstacles and opportunities these churches were experiencing, and what possibilities might emerge for bridge-building with the people of Grace.

It happened. A collegian from Grace went to Kenya to teach for a year. An Indian pastor spent 10 months with us as pastor-in-residence, and lay leaders from congregations in South India visited Grace. One of our medical students went to Nepal to assist as a summer intern in a medical mission in Katmandu. Two seminarians from the Anglican Chinese University of Hong Kong spent summer internships at Grace in separate years. Our parish support for Christ's global mission increased to churches, schools, and individuals in Palestine, Kenya, India, and Nepal. My own expanded vision of the breadth and length of the kingdom in today's world found its way into more sermons, confirmation classes, adult-education courses, pastoral calls, and living-room conversations than I can recount.

A second sabbatical came 10 years later in 1993 and took me to contacts with congregations in New Zealand, Australia, and Papua New Guinea, and later to retreat centers in Taizé, France, and Iona, off the west coast of Scotland. Among the many learning experiences these sabbaticals afforded me, the blessing that runs through them all is the Christian hospitality received in every place.

The rhythms of parish life took on new meaning during my sabbatical absence from Grace. Pastoral associates served the congregation effectively while I was away for several months, giving both people and pastors opportunity to appreciate each others' gifts at deeper levels. And for one who served a long pastorate at Grace it brought the reminder that the life of the parish flows on well without me. I came back refreshed and broadened in my work after seeing firsthand the joys and burdens Christians experience elsewhere in the world. As a result of sabbatical contacts, the exchange of laity and clergy between Grace Church and congregations afar enabled people in both places to see new ministries with new eyes. Those who had never traveled widely gained more of a grasp of the global scope of the gospel through overseas visitors.

The blessings of sabbatical experiences still come back to me whenever I sing a verse of a favorite evening hymn with its simple, powerful image of God's people worldwide:

> The sun, here having set, is waking
> Your children under western skies,
> And hour by hour, as day is breaking,
> Fresh hymns of thankful praise arise.

John Ellerton, 1826–1893, "The Day Thou Gavest, Lord, Is Ended," text alt., in *Lutheran Book of Worship* (1978).

Silence

A guest pastor from India commented after a Sunday service at Grace: "Dear brother, your beautiful Sunday worship service began with singing 'Let all mortal flesh keep silence,' followed by 60 minutes of uninterrupted speech." He caught the irony of what we missed, our singing about awe-filled silence before

God and our structured avoidance of doing so. Our American culture is hardly fertile soil for cultivating spiritual depth. We Christians reflect a general impatience with anything that doesn't jump from one subject to another, without time for silence in between. I am told that the average American has an attention span of 22 seconds. We need help in learning to receive silence as a gift in the rhythms of worship and the daily life of faith.

I tried to offer some of that needed help one Sunday morning by beginning a sermon in a manner unlike any before—or since. I entered the pulpit and stood silent for a full 90 seconds. People were polite at first, thinking that a few seconds' initial pause was to gain attention. Thirty seconds in, the mood began to change, some congregants simply bewildered, others unamused, thinking this was a ruse to test their patience. At the one-minute point the restlessness gave way to worry that I might be having a stroke or a premature senior moment. After 90 seconds, which seemed to me and to everyone else an eternity, I explained the intentional silence as an introduction to a sermon on Psalm 46:10 and the divine command: "Be still and know that I am God." Once was enough for that way of teaching silence by springing it on the congregation as a surprise. I did not use it again. We Americans are used to having virtually every waking moment filled with sound. Thus our discomfort with silence is predictable. I used to think it was a generational matter that I could never understand why our kids as teenagers put on some heavy-metal rock as background noise while doing homework. But I'm convinced that all of us of all ages are so conditioned by the technologies of sound production that the image of the human head with earphones is the sign of our times. We come as moderns ill-prepared to accept silence, in the sense of something other than the absence of sound, as an essential in how we relate to God.

That we are accustomed to nearly constant sound poses a tough challenge in making room for silence in the rhythms of worship and life. Silence must be consciously sought, prepared for, and received with an awareness of what to do with it. A step in the right direction appears more often these days in worship bulletins. "Silence for reflection" is a welcome invitation, and worshipers understand and make good use of it. It's a small but hopeful sign of providing perhaps 60 seconds of silence for thinking, meditating, praying in response to the Word proclaimed. Are there other times and ways in which silence can be balanced with sound in a healthy rhythm? I am a novice with much to learn. I have found, however, that when taking a walk I can turn off distracting sounds and fill silence by drawing from a treasury of memorized hymn verses and favorite passages of Scripture that turn me to God for the sheer enjoyment of his presence. Another opportunity comes when time otherwise lost to frustration because of unexpected delays can be turned into time for quiet while waiting.

An example comes to mind from a call I made at a hospital some distance away. The parishioner I visited died while I was there. She was a widow with an adult son who was on a four-hour flight in the hope of seeing his mother before she died. I wanted to be present when he arrived and found an empty hospital room where I could wait for him. That meant spending four hours in silence, remembering the varied experiences throughout my life and the goodness of God that had brought me to the present. It turned out to be a wonderful four hours, beyond anything I had expected. When the son arrived, I was grateful to keep the flow of thought and prayer moving, this time in ministry to one grieving the death of his mother. It was a forceful reminder to me that silence can be the best preparation for speaking the Word of faith. While I respect the Trappist tradition of round-the-clock silence, I am too immersed in the tradition of Martin Luther with emphasis on the congregation as a "mouth house" ever to leave it.

Here it must be said, however, how thin Lutheran and other Protestant traditions are in cultivating the inner spiritual life and the place of silence. We must go back to 17th-century German pastoral theologians such as Johannes Bengel and Matthias Claudius for sources of a tradition that consciously cultivates the life of the soul. Another notable figure from that era is Martin Rinkart, whose magnificent hymn "Now Thank We All Our God" was written during the plague that swept away his family as well as most of the faithful in the place where he served. Who knows the hours of silence and sorrow that produced such a hymn? It's worth noting that these were parish pastors who were silent before God and therefore had something lasting to say. In more recent times the pastor and martyr Dietrich Bonhoeffer's letters from prison are classics of the inner life. He filled the silence of his prison cell with the profound faith expressed in his poems and prayers, a faith that a Nazi hangman's noose could not defeat. We in our American activist setting are tempted daily to measure ministry more by quick success than by spiritual qualities that take time and silence to develop.

We do well to reclaim the Sabbath from what the world has made it as a sacred gift for nourishing the inner life. Keeping Sabbath is surely a countercultural activity, a subversive rebellion against the forces that march us pell-mell through weekend distractions, bringing us to Monday morning drained instead of refreshed. Somewhere I read a reminder about Genesis 2:1–4, pointing out that God's rest occurred in the context of his creating. God stopped making, stopped speaking, stopped doing, to enjoy his much-doing. I can best speak to what that means for the pastor's Sunday by remembering how it was after the sermon was preached, the sacraments administered, the service concluded, the parishioners greeted, and the remaining details taken care of before I headed home. At home came moments of savoring in my own soul the Word proclaimed to others. Martin Luther wrote of his routine in this respect; stopping for a glass of ale on the way home from the Castle Church in Wittenberg, he would return to the hubbub of the Luther household and enjoy it all—"while the Word did its work." For me a glass of wine did the trick as the Word I preached did its work. I could go home from church, relish table fellowship and converse with the family about morning worship and much else, and, *Deo gratias,* take an afternoon nap. These quiet spaces were and remain gifts of time filled with the warmth of hospitable love and thus quiet in the sense of space opened to grace. They are precious in the rhythms of pastoral life, and every pastor needs them in some form.

If hell is noise, as C. S. Lewis averred, then silence is golden and much more. It is a gift for our taking. As a community and as individuals, we experience its highest purpose when God fills it with the Word of Christ and the wondrous mystery of the Paraclete's indwelling. From that prime purpose of giving God a hearing, silence spreads its leavening effect to every aspect of pastoral ministry.

I choose one example that may seem lightweight at first, but it is a small matter that points to a large matter. I call the place where I do my work a study, not an office. Study is not the only thing I do there, but it is a main thing. When I need the study for study, I close the door for quiet, turn off the phone, gather the tools I need, and devote myself to study. Silence is the *sine qua non* for this essential in my ongoing calling. Being gone from home much of the time now in travel overseas makes it harder to concentrate without the benefit of a study, but there is still no substitute for solitude wherever I can find it to think and write.

In my pastoral days at Grace I was the beneficiary of a tradition that honors continuing graduate education, which has been encouraged by the congregation for Grace's pastors for more than 80 years. When combining part-time graduate study with full-time pastoral work, all of us soon discovered that it was late evening on most days when time was finally available to get at assignments. Those hours, as I recall, were indeed quiet hours, necessarily so. Solitude for scholarship has a long tradition in the church and beyond it, with exemplars who were often burdened with huge schedules and constant demands. An example is from the mystic St. John of the Cross: "The Father uttered one Word; that Word is his Son and he utters him for ever in everlasting silence; and in silence the soul has to hear it." (And from a very different source is Abraham Lincoln's wry observation, "Better to remain silent and be thought a fool than to speak out and remove all doubt.") I have learned from the late Henri Nouwen about silence needed not only for thinking but for allowing the descent of the mind's devotion to the deeper recesses of the heart. He wrote a little classic on that work of the Spirit after spending hours sitting alone before Rembrandt's masterpiece in St. Petersburg's Hermitage Museum, based on Jesus's parable of the prodigal son. I had that opportunity when teaching in that city; sitting in silence before that great sermon on canvas was not so much an activity of the mind as it was a feast for the soul. Some central themes of the faith—sin with its impoverishing effect, repentance as a turning around of life, the Father's costly grace, the unforgiving older brother in the shadows—moved from my head to my heart as I sat for hours where Nouwen had before he wrote *The Return of the Prodigal Son*. One need not go to the Hermitage for the experience; Nouwen brings it close with classic brevity. Without such reverent quiet before God, expressed in different ways and places, our ministries cannot be as deep and enduring as they are meant to be.

The gifts disclosed through moments of silence can come unexpectedly. I remember times when, as I hustled down the hallway outside my study on my way somewhere, my eye caught the rich, deep blues, greens, reds, and golds pouring through the stained-glass windows from the late-morning sun to make a stunning splash of color on the slate floor of the Grace sanctuary. The effect made me stop and savor the beauty waiting there in the quiet of the empty sanctuary (why empty so much of the week?) and offered me an unexpected gift, in Technicolor no less! Like divine grace itself, these are moments we don't create. We receive them. Willingness to recognize them and openness to receive them are our part in the connection. I have found that the universe still holds together if such moments are not lost to schedule anxiety. Other numinous glimpses of God's grandeur come to mind: the late-afternoon sun breaking through blue-black clouds as a storm passes by; the glisten of sunlight on a patch of dew-covered grass, just turned green with springtime freshness; the almost audible silence of the sheer magnificence of the Grand Canyon. These remembered moments come from

God's work in nature. Even more filled with wonder is his work through people, who over time are being changed from one degree of glory to another (2 Cor. 3:18) by the Lord Christ, who made time for silence and prayer in preparation for sharing with us the glory of his redeeming love.

As I continue to seek and find silence and blend it into the rhythms of the daily rounds, I share an Advent prayer often attributed to Dame Julian of Norwich, that 14th-century woman whose writings during her brief life still speak to us across the centuries:

> Lord, let not our souls be busy inns that have no room for
>   thee or thine,
> But quiet homes of prayer and praise, where thou mayest
>   find fit company,
> Where the needful cares of life are wisely ordered and put
>   away,
> And wide, sweet spaces kept for thee; where holy thoughts
>   pass up and down
> And fervent longings watch and wait thy coming.

Growth

Like most kids, I suppose, I kept track of my physical growth by making pencil marks on the kitchen door-frame in our house. It was in the summer of my 14th year, I think, that nearly a half-foot separated the pencil marks. Spiritual growth, like physical growth, comes in spurts at times.

Growth in the art and skills of pastoral ministry has a similar pattern. I think of the early, formative periods of rapid growth: my seminary years, the two years of vicarage (internship) in Japan, graduate study at the University of Chicago, and most of all, the years of my pastorate at Grace Lutheran Church.

How is it that such a mysterious thing as spiritual growth takes place? Nearly every answer that pertains to clergy seems to derive from the daily rounds of serving people in the congregation. Pastoral counseling is one area of growth that has continued through the years. It was enhanced by a fruitful association with an area professional worth commenting on, Richard Matteson. A psychologist and an ordained United Methodist minister, Matteson is well trained for his specialized vocation in helping adults and youth sort out and deal with problems that make life dysfunctional. He invited clergy in our community to come together informally to get acquainted and explore how we might help each other. I found the session intriguing. It began a long and fruitful association and friendship. In pastoral counseling with people, I would come across clinical problems beyond my scope and would recommend that people meet with Dick. He, in turn, would recommend people to me who were navigating stormy waters with no spiritual rudder. We would meet for lunch every several weeks to help each other better understand those we were counseling, always with the permission of the people involved. The mutual benefit we each experienced expanded beyond our personal link. Richard Matteson has taught numerous adult-education classes at Grace and is widely respected in our parish. I don't know why more clergy do not avail themselves of such beneficial partnerships. Counseling may not be the gift every pastor possesses, but in my case I have grown through this partnership of mutual respect.

I have grown in the art of preparing couples for marriage. In my first years at Grace, marriage preparation was limited to meeting with the couple for wedding details and some conversation about their readiness for the rest of their lives together. It soon became obvious that much more was needed. Learning much from listening to prospective married couples, I wrote a manual that set out basics of the unity shared by husband and wife in mind, body, and soul, based on the foundation of the self-giving love of Christ for us. I ask them to read it aloud, page by page, to each other. The material is interspersed with questions, intended to encourage the couple to lay aside the manual and tailor the particular subject to their own needs and interests at this stage of their preparation. Premarital preparation meetings expanded to three, sometimes four or more, as the need dictated. Throughout these decades of preparing couples for marriage at Grace Church, the divorce rate in the nation moved from one to two out of every three marriages. I had no choice but to seek far more effective ways of preparing couples for their Christian calling as husband and wife.

Growth has come to me through dealing with conflict. The difficult years of struggle between congregation and denomination were nonetheless years of growth. Above all, growth, much greater than the pain of its circumstances, came about through standing up for the gospel and taking the consequences. Bad as those years were, I would not have missed for anything the growth that comes only by trusting divine grace to work for good in all things.

Growth has come through advocating the wider role of women in all aspects of Grace Church. Leadership in the congregation was very much a man's world when I began in 1954. I marvel at the ways we all have grown in recognizing the implications of Galatians 3:28 for our time and place ("There is no longer Jew or Greek, there is no longer slave or free, there is no longer male and female; for all of you are one in Christ Jesus"). Now women serve according to their gifts, including pastoral gifts, and we are the richer for it.

We have grown through greater use of the rich liturgical heritage of the church, as well as new hymns and liturgy that bear the mark of biblical soundness and musical excellence. Introducing a new liturgy and hymnal came during a time in the 1980s when doing so was more often a battle than an experience of growth. It would have been inexcusable arrogance for me to have throttled the exceptional gifts of church musicians Paul Bouman, Richard Hillert, Carl Schalk, Harriet Ziegenhals—all Grace members who have written hymn tunes and liturgies that are used in our parish, throughout the Lutheran Church, and across the whole spectrum of Roman Catholic and Protestant churches in and beyond America. I grew as I listened to them, learned from their high standards of musical excellence and theological content. And I grew by enjoying their gifts incorporated into the *Lutheran Book of Worship*, which Bouman and

Schalk helped introduce in brief comments at the beginning of worship through a series of 12 weeks. No aspect of my growth has been more enjoyable!

Growth continues. The transition from the Grace pastorate to emeritus status and the continuing ministry of teaching and mentoring overseas have written another chapter of undeserved grace in my life. What better way to grow, I ask myself, than to share with younger men and women what I have been given at Grace?

The rhythms of the pastoral calling flow on. For me, the grace in that ongoing current has brought surprises and satisfactions. When I stepped down as pastor in 1998, the children of the parish gave me pictures they had drawn and messages of their good will. Among my most cherished is one from a seven-year-old who wished me well as I was entering my "retardement"—a lovely near-miss—but the experience of growth continues to be anything but. Soon a decade will have passed since my stepping down at Grace, into post-retirement teaching ministries in Eastern Europe and Africa. I have learned new things about the rhythms of pastoral ministry by listening to stories told by older clergy in Slovakia, Romania, and Russia. They told of being accused of political treason by their communist governments and arrested, imprisoned, and tortured; some had memories of clergy executed for the sake of the gospel. Others recalled worship and preaching interrupted by police at the door, who emptied the sanctuary, then burned it down or turned it into a granary, dance hall, or museum of atheism. Since the fall of communism in these lands, pastors have had to begin from scratch in finding new ways to reach generations with little or no Christian memory. Teaching opportunities in Africa have introduced me to pastors whose ministries seem to have no everydayness or anything resembling a sabbatical. Their pastoral rhythms are carried out in the face of staggering problems—pandemic AIDS; constant, grinding poverty; and the blight of political and ecclesial corruption. Yet they worship, sing, pray, and continue to serve, carried by the rhythms of grace that are their strength. Surely one of the finest things that can happen in our time is bridge-building that joins us across barriers of every kind in growing together toward the greater fullness of the church, the body of Christ in the world.

6

The Grace of It All

HOW CONGREGATIONS ARE NAMED OFTEN OFFERS AN interesting commentary on what their founders believed (or sometimes, the location where their believing took place). I wish we knew more about how the name Grace was chosen when our congregation was formed over a century ago. All we know from the sketchy record of our beginnings is that several dozen charter member families met on a Sunday afternoon in March 1902, resolved to start a new congregation, chose Grace as a name, and that was that. It's not surprising. Among the thousands of Lutheran congregations in the United States, Grace is among the half-dozen names most frequently chosen. Our bias is understandable. For heirs of Martin Luther, grace says it all—God's undeserved love for us has been given to us through the cross and resurrection of Jesus his Son. What matters, of course, is what goes on under the name over the church door. If grace is at least partially recognizable in who we are and what we do together, we're not misnamed. Grace is truly amazing as it weaves its way like a golden thread through our ups and downs, constantly filling the gaps where we've fallen short and growing us together into the fullness of Christ's stature. One looks back and can't help but marvel at the grace of it all!

Satisfaction

Satisfaction in the work of pastoral ministry doesn't come when we make it into a hefty salary bracket or acquire social prestige.

This is not to justify low pay or to minimize the importance of our calling.

Pastors find satisfaction in a multitude of ministerial experiences. Sometimes satisfaction is wonderfully present in a given moment: confirming a mentally handicapped youth, receiving a good-news letter from a long-lost parishioner, hearing any and all sermon feedback affirming that the Word is at work, spending an Easter Monday doing nothing to the glory of God. Then there are the enduring satisfactions that come over time: preaching the Word in season and out of season, seeing those once shallow in faith come at last to spiritual maturity through "sustaining with a word those that are weary" (Isa. 50:4), praying a congregation into a broader vision of God's mission worldwide, developing a youth ministry that really engages kids. These can sometimes take a half-century—I speak from experience—to emerge full-blown. They affirm the whole experience of ministry itself as deeply satisfying, crowned as it is by Christ's grace. In the long view I find that these satisfactions outrank all other compensations in the calling, whether money or security or status. They are modern versions of what Paul the apostle knew as the good fight well fought, the race finished, the faith kept, and the forward look to the crown of righteousness upon all who long for Christ's appearing. Pastoral theologian Richard Lischer calls these benefits *Open Secrets*, an apt title for the eloquent memoir of his first call among earthy Lutherans in a rural Midwestern parish. To regard people, ourselves included, as open secrets is to see them as epiphanies (*epiphany* means "revealing what lay hidden") of grace, examples of the Lord making saints out of sinners, building his church from the improbable candidates for holiness that we are. Satisfaction comes from taking part in the miracle that by its very makeup every congregation is.

Such benisons are not to be taken for granted, given the ways satisfactions can fade or be lost altogether despite the best of intentions. I saw what the absence of rewarding occasions did to Stan, a friend and pastor of gentle disposition, faithful in his pastoral work. Over 30 years ago our paths crossed. He stayed in our home for a time while we tried to match him up with a fine woman my wife knew. As much as he wanted the satisfactions of a happy marriage, he had no heart or energy left to find it after mean-spirited people had worn him out in the troubled congregation he was serving. Finally he left the pastoral ministry and died much too early of a broken heart. Surely some affirmation of his gifts, some satisfaction in using them, could have sustained him through a hard time and encouraged him toward trying to find romance and marriage. It didn't happen.

Inexcusably poor financial support, loneliness, or strife in family life are other burdens that can blot out needed satisfactions. When pastoral colleagues, women and men alike, suffer these things and slip from view with few knowing or caring, a judgment falls on all of us who fail in our collegial responsibilities as fellow members of Christ's body.

But when our eyes are opened by grace to the satisfactions that bless our days, their abundance is multiplied by sharing them. My awareness of the importance of such sharing began in my first several years as an assistant at Grace under a senior pastor who made it a point to share his pastoral satisfactions with me. He told me stories about the positives he learned while shepherding the congregation through the minefield of a language change, from German to English, in a rocky first decade of his Grace ministry. That was followed by the huge task of keeping the financial support coming to pay for the splendid new church and school building through the Great Depression of the 1930s. And then came the World War II years and ministry to families whose soldier sons never came back. Because he practiced the grace that he preached, he modeled for me the satisfactions of his ministry that were doubled as he passed them on. His 40-year pastorate at Grace was tested by much that could have quenched his buoyant spirit and left him drained and bitter. But the Holy Spirit carried him through all that was vexing and wearisome by keeping his life and work centered on the cross. Knowing something of what he had been through, I sensed the authentic ring in his witness and found it hopeful and beckoning.

I wish that encouraging experience for every pastor, whether beginning or well along in years of service. We need each other's stories of satisfactions in the work. The disappointments, like the poor, we have always with us. But the good news of Christ's grace abounds over sin and brings the great gain of godliness with contentment. That phrase, by the way, "godliness with contentment," might sound slightly, or hugely, out of sync with what registers with sophisticated moderns. But what it stands for never goes out of style. The deep-down fulfillment that comes in serving God and his people in the church and world is of surpassing worth, second to none.

Hope

We Americans are good at optimism. It shows in service and voluntary organizations of many kinds. The Optimist Club of America, one of numerous service organizations with a can-do spirit of supporting good causes, opens its weekly meetings by having its members pledge anew "to be too large for worry, too noble for anger, too strong for fear, and too happy to permit the presence of trouble." There is much to admire in those good intentions.

Yet I confess to an ambivalence about the view of optimism the Optimists describe. We still have human sin to deal with. Optimism won't suffice when the chips are down at three o'clock in the morning in a hospital critical-care unit and the machine that monitors brain waves shows death on the move. It's true that being around optimistic people beats being around perpetual grumps, but optimism is no real cure for the deep human longings for more than a sunny disposition.

I bank on hope as more than optimism. The late theologian Jaroslav Pelikan described the difference in a provocative sentence I remember from a seminary class with him years ago:

"Christians are pessimistic about man but optimistic about God and therefore hopeful for the future." In 15 words he distinguished hope from lightweight optimism and anchored it securely in God as a theological virtue that can outlast whatever beats against it in a fallen world. That truth comes through more fully in one of Paul's most tightly packed sentences:

> We also boast in our sufferings, knowing that suffering produces endurance, and endurance produces character, and character produces hope, and hope does not disappoint us, because God's love has been poured into our hearts through the Holy Spirit that has been given to us"
>
> Romans 5:3–4

It's worth noting how Paul put that claim about hope to work in dealing pastorally with a staffing problem encountered during his missionary apostolate. In preparing for his second missionary journey, Paul locked horns with Barnabas over whether to include John Mark—the young man who for some reason had left Paul and their work midway into the first missionary journey. The conflict over Mark became so heated that Paul and Barnabas split. Barnabas took John Mark and went to Cyprus for continuing mission. Paul chose Silas and set out for Asia Minor and eventually Greece. Years later, when Paul wrote to the Colossian congregation the epistle that bears some of his most exalted witness to the towering sufficiency of Jesus as the Christ of God, he added a personal note of greeting and mentioned Mark, the onetime source of sharp conflict. His fascinating postscript says the Colossians should receive John Mark as one who had been a comfort to Paul (Col. 4:10–11). Hope shines through in that brief instruction. It shows in pastoral practice the power of the hope to overcome the breakup of apostolic partners and implies a later reconciliation between Paul and Mark. Hope builds character, Paul had preached in Romans 5—in this case, Paul's own character, which needed rescue from knee-jerk judgments about suitable partners for ongoing mission. Hope is celebrated as the gift of the God of hope (Rom. 15:13), whose Spirit fills believers with joy and peace in hope abounding.

Hope has been the signature theme of theologian Jurgen Moltmann, whose books have made an impact on clergy and laity worldwide in recent decades. While I am grateful to be among those who have read him with benefit, I join most pastors in citing the parish itself as a living theological textbook on hope. We see it working in those who hang on in hope against the odds. Faces come to mind.

I see June Froehlig, a parishioner I have known and admired for more than 35 years. Her husband, always present with her in worship and quick to volunteer his electrician skills when needed, died of a massive heart attack just as he was approaching midlife. June was left to steer her family of five children through the craziness of the drug culture and the rebelliousness of the early 1970s. One of her adult sons was killed by an gasoline truck that exploded into flames when it crashed into the vehicle he had stopped along the roadside to repair. Another son, the oldest and mainstay of the family after her husband's death, died after a long bout with cancer. Like the countless faithful schooled in life's harsh realities, June knows that in the army of the Lord, the wounded veterans serve best, are least given to loveless judgments, are most ready to go the second mile, are there when needed. Her Unsinkable-Molly-Brown quality suggests another symbol for hope besides the traditional anchor—a cork. She embodies the many who are walking sermons on faith and its fruit of hope that endures when lesser hopes fade, a Christ-given hope that holds through every storm.

Andrew Prinz is a very different person who yet embodies the virtue of hope. He's brainy, a college professor, upbeat but not bubbly, tough-minded but tenderhearted, sober about the urban issues he teaches but steady in his insistence on connecting Christian faith to political responsibility. He has taught frequent parish adult-education sessions that sharpen our awareness of problems ranging from state-sponsored gambling to political resistance to campaign finance to the scandal of our prison system. He encouraged me to go in person with my dissent over our nation's intervention in Vietnam to Congressman Henry Hyde in his suburban Chicago office. I did so. The meeting was memorable, because it taught me how intractable lawmakers can be when they equate American honor with firepower that incinerates civilians as well as enemy troops. Don't expect to win in such discussions, Andy cautioned. Get directly to the point, state your case, and leave with a prayer of hope in your heart that God will do something with your effort. Andrew Prinz is a treasure in the congregation because he keeps pointing us to the hope of God's action in the public sphere, where Lutherans have been slow to recognize God's sovereignty at work. More recently his witness has been deepened as he pits the hope inspired by the gospel against the brain cancer he is battling.

Karen Kress, now in her 36th year of battling multiple sclerosis, is a Stephen minister—a congregation-based program of providing spiritual support for people who welcome it. She is a model of hope to those she reaches with her warmth of spirit and quiet words of faith spoken from her motorized wheelchair. I remember Karen Mitterer from her elementary school days, plucky and cheerful despite a debilitating disease that stunted her growth but not her hope for using her gifts in a vocation of public service. She is now a defense lawyer in Los Angeles who brings stories of hope for defeated people whenever she returns to visit us at Grace.

Robert Busse had to give up teaching piano on a university faculty after suffering a debilitating stroke. Though his gifted hands were no longer able to play Schumann and Bach, he mastered the art of tatting and has made beautiful altar coverings, especially colorful for festival seasons of the church year. I see them as signs of hope that in discovering other talents and using them, Robert found that his life had meaning despite the loss of his principal talent as a teacher of music.

Paula Zwintscher, nearly sightless now that she has reached her 90s, is no longer able to sing in the senior choir, but she can still write letters of hope to Paul Eichwedel, a Grace parishioner now in his 20th year as a state prison inmate. Paul, whose name is included in every Sunday worship bulletin as one for whom we pray, answers Paula's letters with frequent reference to how essential it is that people like Paula sustain him in hope amidst all the forces of prison life that make a mockery of hope. I think of parents who have outlasted long-term problems with their children that had sometimes exploded into knock-down fights at home, by persevering in hope and prayer for their sons and daughters to find purposeful lives. It is even more amazing when children take on adult responsibilities as beacons of hope, at a time when their parents are adrift in alcoholism or infidelity or indifference to the most elemental responsibilities of providing for their children.

When it comes to pastoral examples of hope on an international scale, I treasure the experience of a week with Mitri Raheb, pastor of Christmas Lutheran Church in Bethlehem, a few minutes' walk from the Church of the Nativity, built over the grotto where Jesus traditionally is thought to have been born. He is in his mid-40s, slight of build, wiry. His face is friendly, and his eyes have a penetrating intensity. His quick step is well suited to his boldness in confronting the constant challenge of keeping hope alive among his Palestinian parishioners, surely among the most beleaguered in the world. The Israeli-built wall of separation, 26 feet high and several feet thick, twists like a snake through Bethlehem and beyond, throughout the Israeli-occupied territories. It is a depressing symbol of the hopelessness that hangs over the 70,000 Arabs in Bethlehem, mostly refugees who have lost properties, houses, businesses, schools, and freedom to travel outside Bethlehem for things as basic as a medical prescription, emergency hospital care, or a visit to family or friends.

I met Pastor Raheb at a conference of several hundred clergy and laity from abroad, one of many he plans and leads to work for peace in the Holy Land. I spoke with him in his office at the International Conference Center, an impressive multistory building adjoining Christmas Lutheran Church. He named hope as first among the needs of his parishioners, fellow Palestinians, and Israeli friends across the border who actively work for peace. When I asked what keeps him from going crazy under incessant pressures, he answered, smiling, "I start a new project!" New projects have included a first-class high school where several hundred Christian and Muslim students learn side by side, the International Conference Center where we were meeting, ongoing conferences that bring people to Bethlehem from all parts of the world, and a regular stream of articles and books combining theological aptitude with cultural and political insight on life between Israeli military occupation from without and Islamic terrorism from within.

On the final day of the conference, Pastor Raheb did two things that demonstrate hope in action. He told us to relax and enjoy the sufficient grace of God, lest we go home overwhelmed by conference resolutions and aspirations in the face of intractable challenges. Then he gave us all shovels and led the way outside to plant trees on a hillside overlooking the high school, as an act of hope for a better future. I think of Pastor Mitri Raheb when hearing the near-constant bad news from the Middle East in general and the Israeli-Palestinian conflict at the heart of it all. He is a pastor to emulate as a witness to God, "who calls into existence the things that do not exist," who inspires his servants to hope against hope, as did the patriarch Abraham when anchored in the divine hope that outlasted all lesser hopes (Rom. 4:17–18).

Dreams

Only once in my life have I dreamed a dream and come to believe it was sent from God. *Once.* Biblical figures received dreams from the Almighty all the time. But I am not in that league. My onetime encounter with the real thing does not qualify me as a theological dream expert, now or ever. But this did happen and I bear witness to it as a decisive event in my pastoral life.

The dream of which I speak has a background. In the early 1970s, Beverly and I purchased land for a getaway place on

Detroit Island, Wisconsin, an idyllic property just off the Lake Michigan shoreline. One summer day in 1973, a friend and I crossed the channel to nearby Washington Island, our larger and more populated neighbor a mile or so to the north, curious to have a look at a spectacular house going up that was the talk of the island. What stayed with me was the sight of magnificent redwood beams arching over the spacious interior, just beginning to take shape. We saw, admired, and left. But a strong impression remained. Eventually the house was completed and passed through several owners in the 20 years following.

In the spring of 1993, I was on a month's sabbatical in Europe, visiting retreat ministries at Taizé in France and elsewhere. My last stop was Iona, a small island of considerable significance in church history since AD 563, when St. Columba reached its shores as an exile from his native Ireland. Years before, I had read about Iona, a retreat center then recently restored to use by George F. McLeod and others from the Church of Scotland. The week there surpassed all expectations. The rich combination of a storied past, the ruins of the 12th-century Franciscan abbey, the rebuilt retreat house, the bracing air and the striking beauty of treeless Iona with its lone peak, scattered sheep pastures, and charming village made strong impressions on Beverly and me. The retreat week was a balance of worship, study, fellowship, quiet, and pilgrimage walks along paths and shores that held countless secrets from 16 centuries of history.

On the night before our departure, I had a dream. In it, I saw the Washington Island house being used as a retreat house for Grace Church. The dream was vivid enough to awaken me. I sat straight up in bed and aroused Beverly to tell her a dream I didn't want to forget. She wondered why the dream could not have waited till dawn for comment; but she listened, nodded in agreement that it was an interesting idea, and went back to sleep.

Upon returning home, I tested my Iona dream by describing it to people I trusted to know the difference between a significant dream and a pipe dream. No one suggested the latter, but neither did I find ready takers of the challenge to fund the